Edwin Corydon Crawford

Civil Government of Illinois and the U.S.

Special Chapters on Chicago and Cook County

Edwin Corydon Crawford

Civil Government of Illinois and the U.S.
Special Chapters on Chicago and Cook County

ISBN/EAN: 9783744783729

Printed in Europe, USA, Canada, Australia, Japan

Cover: Foto ©Suzi / pixelio.de

More available books at **www.hansebooks.com**

CIVIL GOVERNMENT

OF

ILLINOIS AND THE U.S.

SPECIAL CHAPTERS

ON

CHICAGO AND COOK COUNTY

BRIEF HISTORICAL SKETCHES.

BY

EDWIN C. CRAWFORD,

Member of the Chicago Bar.

———

CHICAGO:

GEORGE SHERWOOD & COMPANY.

———

PREFACE.

The objects of this book are :

To describe in detail every part of the machinery of government of the State of Illinois, and of each political sub-division of the State.

. To state briefly all the important duties of every public officer in the State of Illinois.

To outline the government of the United States.

It has been written with especial reference to the wants of teachers and students, and officers of school districts and townships.

It is believed that it will be welcomed by all who desire to be intelligent as to the government in which they are most directly interested, namely, that of their own state, county, township and school district.

E. C. C.

Chicago, October 30, 1882.

PREFACE TO EDITION OF 1890.

The centennial period of the nation has developed new interest in the history of the country.

The brief historical sketches following, have been added to this book to aid in fostering such interest; also, to suggest to Illinois students the importance of their own State's history in relation to that of the other States of the Union.

How to govern cities and other thickly populated districts, wisely, is a question that becomes constantly more important, and more difficult to answer.

It is believed that Chicago and Cook County have attained a degree of efficiency in self-government that will repay careful attention. Hence the addition of the sections following, on the government of Chicago and Cook County.

E. C. C.

Chicago, March 15, 1890.

TABLE OF CONTENTS.

I. THE SCHOOL DISTRICT.

4

GOVERNMENT.

The word **government** means regulation and control. Good government begins within ourselves. If we learn to regulate and control our own thoughts and acts, we shall be fitted to help govern others.

The **first duty** of the citizen is private, and consists in learning to govern himself. His next duty is public. It consists (partly) in voting for good laws and good officers, and in sustaining the officers while they execute the laws.

The **simplest form of civil government** is illustrated by the " Town Meeting." This is an assembly of all the voters of a town, to discuss the business of the town, and enact town laws. Such a government is a **democracy**. [See page 75.]

A **republican government** is one in which laws are made by representatives chosen by those having a right to vote.

A State Legislature, or a City Council, illustrates such a government. [See page 28.]

The government to which we should give most attention (after the government of ourselves), is that of the community in which we live. And we should learn not only its present form and method of operation, but the history of its development from the beginning. Hence, Illinois students of Civil Government should begin with a study of the history of their own state.

HISTORY OF ILLINOIS.

Before the middle of the 17th Century, the **French colonists in Canada** had heard about a great river — the "Messipi," the Indians called it — which it was believed flowed into the Gulf of Mexico, or, perhaps, to Japan or China.

The Indians said its valley abounded in fur-bearing and great numbers of other valuable animals. Thus the French were led to form a strong desire to explore it and barter with the natives for its products.

Authority was obtained from the King of France, Louis XIV, by several persons, to make such explorations.

Among these was **Sieur de LaSalle,** who, in 1671, led the first party into the region now known as the State of Illinois. Entering it at the southern end of Lake Michigan, his party made their way to the Kankakee River, placed their canoes in it and paddled down to the **Illinois River,** and down this, probably, to its mouth.

In 1673, **Marquette and Joliet,** a Jesuit missionary and a trader, ascended the Illinois from the Mississippi to a point about seven miles below the present city of Ottawa, and thence crossed the country to Green Bay.

In 1679, LaSalle again led a party down the Illinois, and, early in 1680, built Fort Crèvecœur and established a colony on the river a short distance from the site of the present city of Peoria.

This was the first civilized settlement made in the territory now composing the State; and it was the beginning of a scheme of colonization, conceived by LaSalle and encouraged by Louis XIV, which was intended to make the whole Mississippi valley tributary to France.

In 1682, LaSalle again descended the Illinois, and also passed down the Mississippi to its mouths. At the beginning of the delta of the Mississippi he erected a column, and, in the name of Louis XIV, took possession of the basin of the great river and its tributaries, naming the region " Louisiana."

On his return, he built a fort at "Starved Rock," on the Illinois, and established a colony there. He also established colonies at Kaskaskia, Cahokia, and other places. He planned to establish a chain of forts and colonies, along the whole extent of the Illinois and Mississippi Rivers, to carry on trade with the Indians, and to secure their alliance against the danger of encroachments by the colonies of England and Holland on the eastern border of the continent.

Other colonies followed those started by LaSalle, till, in the middle of the 18th Century, the Illinois territory contained several thousand French settlers, who were generally in a prosperous condition. Travelers visiting them, on returning to France, called the country "a new Paradise."

But English colonists had come also, and disputes began to arise about boundaries, which led to war between France and England, and at its close, England became owner of a vast region formerly claimed by France, including the territory composing the present State of Illinois.

During the next fifty years most of the new settlers in Illinois came from **Virginia and Kentucky, and from the French settlements on the Mississippi River.** Nearly all of the settlers of this period located in the southern half of the State.

In 1804, Fort Dearborn was built near the mouth of the Chicago River. Burned by Indians during the war of 1812, it was rebuilt in 1816.

About fifteen years later, immigrants began to settle in the northern part of the territory, most of them coming from the Eastern and Northern States.

Illinois, after passing into the possession of England, was considered a **part of Virginia,** and was organized as a county of Virginia in 1778.

In 1787, Virginia ceded to the United States all its land situated northwest of the Ohio River.

The Act of cession is known as the "Ordinance of 1787." One of its provisions was, that slavery should never be permitted in the region ceded.

Congress created the Territory of Illinois in the year 1809.

On the 12th day of February, in the same year, a child was born in a log cabin in Hardin County, Kentucky, who was destined to make the future State famous above all its sisters, as the home of the saviour of the Union and the liberator of a race of slaves. The child was **Abraham Lincoln.**

The northern line of the Territory ran from the southern point of Lake Michigan due west to the Mississippi River. Thus, the Territory was without a harbor.

It was expected, even as early as 1809, that the Federal government would aid in making a canal connecting Lake Michigan and the Mississippi River.

Illinois was admitted to the Union as a State in 1818.

Hon. Nathaniel Pope was its last territorial delegate in Congress. With great wisdom he represented to Congress that if admitted into the Union with its then northern boundary, the State's only outlet for its products would be the Mississippi River; that its commercial interests being thus made identical with those of the territory south and west of it, if ever the Southern or Western States should withdraw from the Union, Illinois would be forced, by commercial causes, to go with them.

But, Mr. Pope argued, if Illinois could have harbors on the Lake, and thus establish trade relations with the Northern and Eastern, as well as the Southern and Western, States, it would be made a powerful agent to prevent the disruption of the Union.

He, therefore, urged Congress to remove the northern boundary to 42½° north Latitude. This provision was accordingly embodied in the act of admission, thus giving to the State the valuable harbors of Chicago, Calumet and Waukegan.

How nobly the State, a half century later, justified

the hope of this far-seeing statesman, is written with
the blood of nearly nine thousand of its sons who, from
1861 to 1865, gave their lives on Southern battlefields
to preserve the Union of all the States.

The new State's* first capital was Kaskaskia, which
had been the center of civil and judicial power since
the time of LaSalle; but the first Legislature provided for removing the seat of government to Vandalia,
the next year.

The State's first Governor was Shadrach Bond,
of Kaskaskia. Its first Congressman was Daniel P.
Cook, for whom Cook County was afterward named.

The first Legislature, in spite of the Ordinance of
1787, passed a law permitting slave-holding to a limited extent; but, in 1824, by a popular vote, slavery
was abolished absolutely.

**In 1818, the State had a population of about
45,000 people.** Of these, about 2,000 were descend-
ants of the French colonists, who LaSalle and his successors had hoped would increase in numbers till they
would fill the Mississippi Valley and become the con-
trolling power of the New World.

The portion of the State north of Alton and Ed-
wardsville was almost wholly destitute of settlers.

Governor Bond and his successor, Governor Coles,
both urged the Legislature to take some action in reference to the proposed **canal connecting Lake Michigan and the Mississippi River.**

Their immediate object was to secure the peopling

---

* The State lies between Latitude 86° 59′ and 42° 30′ north, and
Longitude 87° 35′ and 91° 40′ west. Its extreme length is 385 miles,
and its extreme width 218 miles. Its area is 55,410 square miles.

of the northern portion of the State, by providing it with means of transportation.

A few years later, Congress granted to the State 300,000 acres of land in aid of the canal project; and, on July 4, 1836, work was begun on the canal, and it was finished in 1848.

It starts from the South Branch of the Chicago River and extends to Peru on the Illinois River.

It is not the great ship canal originally planned. But the expectation of such a channel had given a great impulse to the settlement of the northern portion of the State, and railroads soon supplied all that the canal lacked as a means of transportation.

Two years after the completion of the canal, Congress granted to the Illinois Central Railroad Company, land sufficient to provide for the construction of a road running north and south through the central part of the State. This road, finished in 1856, extended from the southern end of the canal to Cairo.

Thus, at last, Lake Michigan and the Mississippi River were connected, and the central part of the State, along the line of the canal and railroad, was rapidly filled with settlers.

In 1831, Black Hawk, a chief of the Sac Indians, and his tribe, who had been transferred beyond the Mississippi, returned to their former location in Illinois. They were joined by the **Fox Indians under their chief, Keokuk.**

A desultory Indian war followed, lasting some months, with the usual incidents of scalping settlers and burning their homes. In July, 1832, the savages were defeated in battle, and Black Hawk and Keokuk captured. This was the State's last experience of Indian warfare.

About 1840 a number of Mormons established themselves at Nauvoo. They organized a government for themselves, independent and in defiance of the laws of the State, procured cannon and small arms, and formed a military force.

Their number increased rapidly. Soon the practice of polygamy was introduced among them.

Joseph Smith, their leader, would not permit officers of the State to perform their duties in Nauvoo. Public feeling became very hostile to the Mormons. Warrants were issued for the arrest of Joseph Smith and his brother Hiram. They surrendered themselves to the authorities, were discharged, but re-arrested on a charge of treason and placed in jail in the town of Carthage to await trial. A mob broke open the jail and murdered them.

During the next two years the country about Nauvoo was almost constantly in a state of great excitement. The number of Mormons had increased to 17,000 people.

They were accused of coining counterfeit money and of stealing property from their non-Mormon neighbors, at every opportunity. Riotous proceedings became frequent.

In the spring of 1846, however, all **the Mormons** but about 1,000 **left the State,** and started for their new home in Utah. Those left behind gave no further trouble.

The State's relation to the Mexican war requires little notice. It contributed its quota of volunteers, six regiments, who served with honor to themselves and credit to the State.

One of the State's later-adopted sons, however, a young second lieutenant in a regiment of regulars, was then receiving his first experience in war, and was unconsciously preparing himself for the great Civil War, in which he was to take the leading part. His name was Ulysses S. Grant.

In 1854, the final contest over the slavery question began. The "Missouri Compromise" Act had been repealed by Congress for the purpose of making Kansas a slave state.

Illinois furnished to the nation **the two chief leaders** of the opposing parties in this contest — **Stephen A. Douglas and Abraham Lincoln.**

Douglas argued that the people residing in any territory ought to be allowed to decide for themselves whether the territory should become a free or a slave state.

Lincoln urged that the whole nation ought to unite in preventing the formation of any more slave states, because slavery was wrong.

In 1860, Lincoln was nominated for President by a convention of the Republican party, meeting in Chicago. The leading principle of the platform was opposition to the spread of slavery.

Douglas was nominated by the Democrat party, on a platform embodying his favorite principle of "Squatter Sovereignty," which was, as stated above, that settlers in the territories should decide the slavery question for themselves.

Thus, as Nathaniel Pope had predicted forty-two

years before, **Illinois took the chief place** in dealing with the subject which involved the question of destroying or preserving the Union.

And when, after Lincoln's inauguration as President, in 1861, the South began war to destroy the Union, Douglas, not less than Lincoln, took his stand for its preservation, and gave to his successful rival and the cause he represented, the most cordial support.

The two parties followed their leaders in the common cause, and the State more than performed its duty in the struggle following.

Under President Lincoln's first call for volunteers, issued April 15, 1861, the quota of Illinois was 6,000 men. Within ten days, more than 10,000 were enlisted.

During the war, the State sent into the Union army 259,092 men. Of these, 5,888 were killed, and 3,032 mortally wounded in battle; 19,496 died of disease, 967 died in Southern prisons, and 205 were lost at sea.

The first great Union victory was won principally by Illinois troops, led by an Illinois General. This was the capture of Fort Donelson with 14,000 Confederate prisoners. The **General was U. S. Grant.**

How General Grant led his soldiers to other victories, was made General-in-Chief of the Union armies, and, with the aid of his brave followers, brought the war to a successful close, can not be told here.

Nor is this the place to narrate President Lincoln's acts during the dark days of the war.

But we may, with just pride, remember that Illinois has given to the nation and the world, the greatest statesman and the ablest general of modern times — Abraham Lincoln and Ulysses S. Grant.

QUESTIONS.

Who was the first explorer of Illinois?

Who the next?

When did they come?

When and where was the first settlement made?

What did LaSalle do on his third visit?

What was the full extent of LaSalle's plan?

What caused war between France and England in the middle of the 18th century?

To what State did Illinois originally belong?

What was the Ordinance of 1787? Its most important provision?

Give an account of the argument of Nathaniel Pope in 1818.

What was the result of it?

How did the State afterward fulfill Mr. Pope's prediction?

The State's first capital? Its second? Its present capital?

The first Governor, and Congressman?

Population of the new State?

First object of the Illinois and Michigan Canal?

Effect of the canal project on the northern part of the State?

Give an account of the origin of the Illinois Central Railroad.

Its effect on settlement?

The Black Hawk war?

Give an account of the Mormon troubles.

What can you say about the State in relation to the Mexican war?

What important question arose about 1854? What two men led in its discussion?

What are some of the things done by Illinois during the Civil war?

THE HISTORY OF CHICAGO.

Chicago is situated at the southern end of Lake Michigan. Its Court House Square is in latitude 41° 52' 20" North, and longitude 87° 37' West from Greenwich. Its elevation above the level of the sea is about 600 feet. Its length on the Lake Shore is 21 miles, its average width about 5 miles, and its territory comprises 164 square miles.

The site of Chicago was first visited by white men in the winter of 1674–5, its visitors being Marquette and Joliet, two French Jesuit missionaries.

In 1795, the first sale of land occurred, the Indians selling to the United States, a "piece of land six miles square at the mouth of the Chekajo River." The first settler arrived the next year, and built a cabin on the north bank of the chief branch of the Chicago River.

A fort named "Fort Dearborn" was built in 1804. It was located just south of the place where Rush Street bridge now stands.

The first business done, was the buying of furs from the Pottawatomie and other Indian tribes.

In 1812, the Indians massacred most of the soldiers in the fort and several settlers, including two women and twelve children, and burned the fort. During the next four years, the place was inhabited only by Indians.

In 1816, the fort was rebuilt, and garrisoned by regular soldiers.

In 1827, the **first slaughterhouse** was built. Archibald Clybourne, for whom a North Side avenue was afterward named, was its proprietor; and he entered upon the business of furnishing meat to the garrison of the fort, and the settlers who then consisted of three families, all living in log houses. Such was the beginning of a Chicago industry which, in its vast extent, is unequaled in any city of the world.

At this time, most of the land where the greatest business houses of the city now stand, was nearly on a level with the lake, and, during the greater part of the year, was little better than a swamp.

The **first map** of Chicago, made in 1830, fixed its **boundaries** as Madison, Desplaines, Kinzie, and State streets.

The **first churches**, a Presbyterian and a Baptist, were established in 1833; also the **first newspaper,** *The Chicago Democrat.*

In the same year, Chicago was **incorporated as a town,** electing four trustees as its governing body.

Seven years later, it became **a city,** with an area of about ten square miles divided into six wards, each of which, as now, elected two aldermen. The population of the new city was 4,170 persons. Of these, about 700 were of school age ; and for these, the city employed two teachers!

Ten years later, the **first railroad** was begun. When finished, it extended from Chicago to Freeport, 121 miles. When it was chartered, in 1836, there were not more than 1,000 miles of railroad in the United States.

In 1850, the city began to use gas for lighting the streets. During the same year a **Board of Trade** was organized.

The first steam grain elevator was built in 1851.

Water Works began to supply houses with water from Lake Michigan in 1854.

During this year the city suffered severely from cholera. Its cause was thought to be the **want of drainage.** Sufficient drainage had been impossible in a great part of the city, because the ground was so nearly level with the Lake. Hence, the city now began to use earth, dredged from the river and thrown out of cellars, to **raise the grade.**

Much of the **present level** of the South Division is five to ten feet above the natural level.

By such filling, perfect drainage became possible, and the **construction of sewers** was carried on rapidly, so that, by the middle of 1857, the thickly-settled parts of the city were well drained.

In May, 1854, Mr. John C. Dore was appointed Chicago's first **Superintendent of Public Schools.** He introduced examinations as a means of determining in what classes pupils should be placed.

A **police force** for day duty, consisting of fifty-four men, was organized in 1855.

The North and South Side **street railways** began to lay rails in 1859. In this year, the **first steam fire engine** was used.

In 1860, the **population** of the city was over 109,000, the **total valuation** of property over $37,-

000,000, and the capital employed that year in handling farm **products** alone, was more than $59,-000,000.

Churches, schools and newspapers had multiplied in proportion to the increase of population and business.

The year 1861 opened on the people deeply absorbed in the countless healthy activities of a young city, already the metropolis of the best agricultural region in the world.

But, on April 14, of that year, word came that the **national flag had been insulted** in Charleston harbor, and a national fort captured by rebels. Then, instantly, **business was forgotten,** and, with it, all other interests save one — **how to preserve the National Union.**

People filled the streets, animated by one feeling — patriotism — and begged that they might be allowed to aid the new President in suppressing the rebellion. On April 19th, Governor Yates called for **volunteer soldiers,** and. at 11 o'clock on the morning of the 21st, **600 men and four cannons** were sent from Chicago in response to the call.

Several thousand other volunteers offered themselves within a few weeks following, whom the government was not then able to accept.

Later, the city was invited to do all it would for the great **cause of freedom and union;** and nobly it responded to the invitation.

Chicago and Cook County together **sent 22,532** men into the Union army during the war, and paid **$62,000,000** of the total expenses of the war.

Chicago's happiest day was April 3, 1865, when it heard that Richmond had been captured by Gen. Grant's army, and its saddest day (before October 9, 1871) was April 19, when it heard of the death of **Abraham Lincoln,** the State's greatest son, and, after Washington, **the nation's greatest benefactor**

The body of the murdered President lay in state in the Court House a day and a night, on its way to interment at Springfield, and an unbroken procession of sincere mourners throughout the night, as well as the day, filed by, to cast a last look upon one whom they had all learned to love as a personal friend.

The year following the close of the war was not a prosperous one for Chicago; but, with 1866, began an era of extraordinary prosperity, which continued, with no sign of decrease, till the terrible night of October 8-9, 1871.

In 1870, the **population was 300,000,** and the trade in materials and manufactured articles received in the city was $400,000,000.

The business of wholesalers was $402,500,000, and that of importers $84,000,000.

The sales of real estate for the year amounted to $42,000,000, the whole valuation of the real estate of the city being about $420,000,000.

The year 1871 brought still greater increase of prosperity. The city's thousand forms of industrial development and pleasure were in the highest state of activity, when, in a night, all development stopped and pleasure ceased. Within two days and nights **forty-five per cent. of the city's wealth** was destroyed, and more than **one-quarter of its people were made homeless.**

The **Great Fire** began at 9 o'clock, P. M., October 8, in a little stable on the West Side; destroyed 500 buildings there; passed over the River to the South Side at midnight, and there destroyed 3,650 buildings. At 3 o'clock A. M., the same night, it descended upon the North Side, and within twenty-four hours, had consumed 13,300 buildings.

When the fire ceased, **$280,000,000 worth** of property had been destroyed, and **98,500 people** made homeless.

The fire had started on Saturday night. On Tuesday following, the **work of resuming business** was begun. The Board of Trade rented a room and began to prepare it for business. Before the end of the day, twelve banks procured temporary quarters, and on Thursday began to pay out money to their depositors.

Rebuilding soon began, and, within three months, a great number of new buildings had been completed, not inferior to those burned. Before three years had passed, nearly the whole of the burnt district was again covered with buildings, most of them superior to those which had been burned.

Much of the reconstructing of the city had to be done, however, on borrowed capital, which it required many years to repay.

Such repayment was made more difficult by the hard times which followed the **"Panic of 1873."** During this period, real estate, especially, depreciated in value, so that, for some years, it could scarcely be sold for any prices, except such as were ruinous to its owners.

This condition continued till about the year 1881, when a new era of prosperity began, which, at this writing (1890), has not closed.

Annexations of territory have been made that swell the city's population to probably 1,200,000.

The estimated value of its business for the year 1889 amounted to $1,177,000,000.

Having thus briefly viewed Chicago's marvelous development, in little more than a **half century,** from a **frontier village** scarcely known outside the county in which it was situated, till it has become a **metropolis** trading with every country of the world, we ought to be interested in learning whether its wonderful territorial ·and commercial growth have been equaled by the development of its civil policy; whether it has produced a form and method of government which furnish to all within its limits, protection in the enjoyment of all their rights.

QUESTIONS.

Define the word government.

What are some of the duties of citizens?

What is the simplest form of government?

What kind of government is a City Council?

What are the latitude and longitude of Chicago, and its elevation above the sea?

When was Chicago first visited by white men?

When did its first settler arrive?

What was Chicago's first business? What its second?

What were Chicago's first boundaries?

When were its first churches and first newspaper established?

When was Chicago first incorporated? When, as a city?

When was the first Chicago railroad begun?

Name Chicago's first Superintendent of Schools.

Give an account of Chicago's part in the Civil War.

Population of Chicago in 1870.

Give an account of the Great Fire of 1871.

Sketch the city's growth since that event.

THE GOVERNMENT OF CHICAGO.

The present **Constitution** of the State of Illinois, adopted in 1870, was framed with the **design of leaving** to the cities of the State, as fully as possible, **exclusive control** of their own affairs.

To this end, the Legislature of the State enacted a a law, which went into effect July 1, 1872, providing for the **incorporation and government** of the cities of the State.

Chicago **became incorporated** under this law by virtue of an election held April 23, 1875.

The **officers** of the corporation of Chicago are: **Mayor, Aldermen, Clerk, Comptroller, Collector, Commissioner of Public Works, Treasurer, Corporation Counsel, City Attorney, Prosecuting Attorney, Health Commissioner, Physician, Superintendent of House of Correction, Sealer of Weights and Measures, Fire Marshal, General Superintendent of Police, Gas Inspector, Inspector of Oils, Inspector of Steam Boilers and Inspector of Fish.**

The **city election** occurs annually, on the first Tuesday in April.

One Alderman is elected every year from each ward, and holds office two years.

Once in two years, a Mayor, Clerk, City Attorney, and Treasurer are elected, for a term of two years.

All the **other officers** named above are **appointed**

by the Mayor, with the consent of the Council, for a term of two years.

The **Legislative Department** of the city consists of the Mayor, the Aldermen, and the City Clerk.

The Mayor and Aldermen compose the **City Council.**

THE MAYOR.

The **Mayor is the chief executive** officer of the city. Some of his duties are:

To preside at the meetings of the Council.

To give the Council, once a year, and oftener if necessary, advice in writing, about the affairs of the city.

To sign ordinances passed by the Council, if he approves them.

To suppress public disorder.

To supervise the conduct of all city officers; and to see that all city ordinances are faithfully executed.

He may vote when a tie occurs, and may veto such ordinances as he disapproves.

An **ordinance vetoed** by the Mayor, **can be passed** by the vote of a majority consisting of two-thirds of the Aldermen.

The **Mayor is assisted** in his personal duties by a Secretary and clerks, appointed by himself, and paid by the city.

THE ALDERMEN.

Chicago is divided into **thirty-four wards,** each of which elects two Aldermen.

An **Alderman** must be a legal voter, and reside in his ward.

While he is an Alderman he **can not hold any other city office,** or be interested in any private business in which money is received from the city.

The **duties of the Council** are:

To take care of the property and finances of the city.

To levy taxes for city purposes.

To borrow money, if necessary, for the use of the city.

To appropriate, annually, a sum sufficient to pay the city's expenses for a year.

To make, improve, and care for, streets, sidewalks, alleys, bridges, parks, etc.

To regulate vessels using the River.

To issue licenses.

To provide for the inspection of food, so that only wholesome food shall be sold.

To provide for extinguishing fires.

To govern the police.

To care for the health of the people.

And to pass all ordinances and rules necessary to carry into effect the powers granted to the city by the Constitution and laws of the State.

The Council can make but one appropriation in a year; and can not **borrow money** exceeding five per cent. of the value of the taxable property of the city, and must provide for the repayment within twenty years of any sum borrowed.

CITY CLERK.

It is the **duty of the Clerk** to keep the corporate seal and all papers belonging to the city; to attend all meetings of the Council and keep a record of its proceedings; and to deliver to the Mayor, ordinances passed by the Council.

The Clerk appoints a **Chief Deputy Clerk**, and is provided with other necessary assistant clerks, such Chief Deputy and assistants being paid by the city.

QUESTIONS.

When did Chicago last become incorporated as a city?

Name its officers. How do they get their offices?

When does the city election occur?

Who are the Legislative Department of the city?

What are the duties of the Mayor?

How can an ordinance be passed over the Mayor's veto?

How many wards in the city?

Qualifications of an Alderman?

Duties of City Council?

Power of the Council to borrow money?

DEPARTMENT OF FINANCE.

This Department has **control of the city's money** — its receipt and expenditure. It embraces the Comptroller, Treasurer, and Collector, and their assistants.

The **Comptroller and Collector** appoint their assistants, with the consent of the Mayor, and the Treasurer appoints his assistants on his own authority.

All such assistants may be discharged by their respective chiefs at any time.

Such power is necessary, because the chiefs are held responsible for the acts of their assistants.

The head of this department is

THE COMPTROLLER.

He has control of all the affairs of the Department. Some of his duties are:

To examine claims against the city for damages to person or property.

To supervise all officers of the city who receive and pay out the city's money, requiring them to report to him monthly, in writing, under oath, all their receipts and disbursements.

To submit the substance of such report to the Council, at its next regular meeting.

The **Comptroller** must also **annually report** to the finance committee of the Council, all **sums of money received and paid out** on the city's account during the preceding year, and **submit** to the Council **estimates** of the probable expenses of the city government during the next year.

The **Mayor must sign,** and the **Comptroller countersign,** all orders on the City Treasurer for money.

THE TREASURER.

It is the **duty of the Treasurer** to receive and safely keep all money belonging to the city, to **pay it out** only on the **order of the Mayor and Comptroller,** and to report, monthly, to the latter, all sums received and paid out during the month preceding.

THE COLLECTOR.

It is his duty to collect license fees and taxes levied as special assessments, and to pay all his receipts, daily, to the Treasurer.

Special assessments are taxes levied for a special purpose, and on property only in a specified part of the city. For example, if a street is to be paved, taxes for such paving levied only on property fronting on such street would be special assessments.

DEPARTMENT OF PUBLIC WORKS.

The **officers** of this department are: **Commissioner of Public Works, his Secretary, City Engineer, Superintendent of Streets, Superintendent of Water, Superintendent of Sewerage, Superintendent of Special Assessments, and Superintendent of Maps.**

The **Commissioner** is the chief officer of the Department. He has power, with the consent of the Mayor, to appoint and remove the other officers of the Department.

Some of his **duties** are:

To have special **charge of all public grounds** of the city, such as streets, sidewalks, parks, etc.; of all **public buildings** belonging to the city; of all the **city lights,** and of the city **Water Works,** including the collection of water rents.

He also has charge of all public improvements, and of special assessments to be levied for the same.

It is his duty to **supervise all the expenditures** made by the Department, and **report annually,** to the Council, all the work done, and the sums of money received and expended by the Department during the year past, and to submit estimates of its probable expenses during the year to come.

It is plain that the Commissioner can not discharge all his duties in person. He has to act mostly through his subordinate officers. His duties are, therefore, divided among them, as follows:

The Commissioner's Secretary attends in the office of the Department during business hours, and has charge of the books and papers of the Department.

The City Engineer has charge of the building and repairing of bridges, viaducts and waterworks, and the laying of public water pipes.

The Superintendent of Streets has charge of the improvement and repair of streets, alleys and sidewalks.

The Superintendent of Water has charge of the collection of water taxes; and it is his duty to pay to the City Treasurer, daily, all such taxes collected.

The Superintendent of Sewers supervises the construction of all public and private sewers and catch-basins.

The Superintendent of Special Assessments has charge of the levying of special taxes on land to pay for public improvements to be made near such land.

The Superintendent of Maps has charge of the records of city maps and plats. and of matters relating to street numbers.

DEPARTMENT OF BUILDINGS.

This is one of the most important departments of the city government. Its officers, (together with the

Superintendent of Sewers and Health Commissioner),
are especially charged with the **care** of the bodily
safety and health of every person in the city.

The **Commissioner of Buildings is its head officer.**
He is assisted by his **Secretary, the Inspector of
Elevators, Inspector of Buildings,** and other employés
of the Department.

It is the **Commissioner's duty** to enforce all ordinances relating to the safety of buildings and elevators, and to prevent the accumulation of combustible
materials where they are liable to produce fires.

Whenever requested by two or more persons, who
state that the **ventilation** of any workshop or factory
is **imperfect,** or that its **doors or stairways are
dangerous** in case of fire, or that its **heating apparatus is unsafe,** the Commissioner must examine such
place, and compel the person in possession to make
necessary changes.

The Commissioner, at least once in six months,
must inspect all **public school buildings, halls,
churches, and theaters,** and all **buildings used for
manufacturing** purposes, to learn whether they are
safe buildings, properly ventilated, used in safe ways,
and capable of allowing a crowd of persons to escape
without injury, in case of fire.

It is also his duty to inspect **buildings while being
erected,** and to see that they are constructed in a safe
manner and according to the city ordinances.

He must investigate the **cause of all fires** that
occur in the city.

The Commissioner's **Secretary** performs duties

similar to those of the Secretary of the Commissioner of Public Works.

The **Inspectors of Buildings and Elevators** must be experienced **architects, builders, or mechanics.** Their duties are sufficiently indicated by their official titles.

QUESTIONS.

Define Department of Finance, and name its officers.

Power of its chief officers?

Their duties?

Officers of Department of Public Works? Their duties?

Who collects water taxes?

Define special assessments.

Why is the Department of Buildings very important?

Name its chief officers?

What are some of the Commissioner's duties?

What are the qualifications of the Inspectors of this Department?

DEPARTMENT OF LAW.

The **Law Department** consists of the **Corporation Counsel, City Attorney, Prosecuting Attorney,** and their assistants.

The head of the Department is the Corporation Counsel.

He superintends, and with the assistance of the City Attorney and City Prosecutor, conducts the city's law business; draws legal papers, when requested by the head of any Department; and furnishes written opinions upon subjects proposed to him by the Mayor, Aldermen, or any of the Departments.

The **City Attorney** assists the Corporation Counsel as directed by the latter; keeps a register of all suits in which the city is a party; and annually reports to the Council what he has done during the year in regard to such suits.

The **Prosecuting Attorney** is required to carry on suits against persons who **violate any city ordinances,** and to prosecute persons charged with crime in the

POLICE COURTS.

The Judges of the Superior, Circuit, and County courts, of Cook County, are required by law, on or before April 1. every fourth year, to send to the Governor of the State, the names of **nineteen men competent** to serve as **Justices of the Peace;** seven for the Town of West Chicago, seven for the Town of South Chicago, and five for the Town of North Chicago.*

These, the Governor is required by law, with the consent of the State Senate, to appoint to such offices.

From these Justices, the Mayor, with the consent of the Council, appoints, biennially, one or more, to

* The three Towns named above, and the Towns of Lake, Hyde Park, Jefferson and Lake View, are within the City of Chicago, and are organized and governed as townships according to the Township Organization Laws of the State. [See page 73 to 86.] At the same time, as portions of the city of Chicago, they are as fully subject to all its laws and ordinances as if they had no township government.

preside over each of the city Police Courts. When so appointed, they are called **Police Magistrates.**

They must hold two sessions of their courts daily, except on Sundays. All persons arrested by the police are brought before a Police Magistrate, who hears the evidence, and, if the prisoner is found guilty, fines him, or commits him to the Grand Jury. [See page 89.]

If the prisoner does not pay his fine, the Magistrate commits him to the House of Correction (commonly known as the Bridewell).

The Mayor may pardon persons thus fined.

Each Police Magistrate is required to keep a record of the cases tried before him, and file it in the Comptroller's office, monthly.

Police Court Clerks and Bailiffs are appointed by the Mayor, with the consent of the Council.

It is the **duty of each Clerk** to keep a full **record of all the cases** tried in the court to which he is assigned, and to **submit** to the Comptroller a **report** of such cases, and **pay to the Treasurer, daily, all** money received.

It is a Bailiff's duty to preserve order in the court.

The prisons to which Police Justices may commit prisoners are the **County Jail and the House of Correction.**

The **Washingtonian Home, Martha Washington Home, House of the Good Shepherd, and Erring Woman's Refuge** are charitable institutions, but they receive certain portions of the city's revenue derived from liquor license fees and fines; and, by consent of their officers, they receive inebriates and erring women who have been found guilty in the Police Courts.

The object of these institutions is to secure the reform of such prisoners.

(The Washingtonian Home receives only male inebriates.)

THE HOUSE OF CORRECTION.

This is the **city prison,** commonly known as the Bridewell. It is situated between Twenty-sixth street and the West Branch of the South Branch of the Chicago River.

It is **under the control** of a Board of **three Inspectors,** appointed by the Mayor, with the consent of the Council.

These Inspectors serve without pay. The Mayor is, **ex-officio,** also a member of the Board.

The Mayor, with the consent of the Inspectors, appoints a Superintendent, who holds his office four years. He must reside at the House of Correction, and give all his time to its affairs.

Prisoners confined in this prison **are required to work** every secular day, and they are **allowed a credit** of fifty cents a day for such work toward the payment of their fines. When the sum of such credits due a prisoner equals his fine and the costs, he is discharged.

QUESTIONS.

Of what does the Law Department consist?

Who is its chief officer?

What are the duties of each of its officers?

How are Justices of the Peace appointed for Chicago?

How do Justices become Police Magistrates?

Duties of Police Magistrates and Police Court Clerks?

To what prisons can such Magistrates commit prisoners?

What is the Bridewell? How is it conducted?

What is the object of the Washingtonian Home?

How may prisoners be discharged from the Bridewell without paying their fines in money?

DEPARTMENT OF HEALTH.

This Department, like that of Buildings, is of the greatest importance to every resident of Chicago, being charged, as it is, with the **duty of preserving the health** of the people of the city.

Its officers are, the **Commissioner of Health, Superintendent of Police, and City Physician.**

The Commissioner has a general supervision of the **City Hospital.**

It is his duty to stop the **progress of all contagious diseases.**

To **quarantine boats and railway trains,** when they are liable to bring contagious diseases into the city.

To vaccinate, without charge, all persons who apply to him.

To cause **nuisances to be removed;** and to do anything else that may be necessary to keep the air of the city pure.

The Commissioner has power to appoint, with the

consent of the Mayor, an **Assistant Commissioner, Secretary,** and a sufficient number of other subordinate officers to enable him to perform the work of his office. On account of the great importance of the duties of his Department, and the fact that he is held responsible for the proper performance of them, he is empowered to discharge any of his assistants, at pleasure.

He is clothed with some other extraordinary powers. If he has reason to believe that there is within a building any cause of disease, he has a right to enter such building, at any hour in the daytime, and take up floors, and use any other necessary means to discover the cause of such disease.

CITY PHYSICIAN.

The City Physician must give medical attendance to patients in the City Hospital, Pest House, Police Stations, and City Prisons, and render assistance to the Commissioner in any other way.

QUESTIONS.

What is the general duty of the Department of Health?

What are some of the Commissioner's especial duties?

His authority over his assistants?

Name some of his powers?

Why is he given extraordinary powers?

Duties of City Physician?

DEPARTMENT OF POLICE.

It is the duty of members of this Department to protect all persons in the city from injury by the disorderly and criminal. Policemen have to deal with not only the worst, but, also, the most unfortunate classes of society.

A good police officer must be a man of courage, intelligence and wisdom; and he must have integrity and kindness.

Chicago has many such police officers. Since the awful **night of May 4, 1886,** the fame of the city's police force, for both courage and moderation, has filled the world.

The Mayor is **commander-in-chief** of the police force; but its **immedia'e head** is

THE SUPERINTENDENT OF POLICE,

Who is commonly known as the Chief, and who appoints all the officers and members of the Department, with the consent of the Mayor.

Members of the Police Force, below the Chief, are are ranked as **Inspectors, Captains, Lieu'enants, Sergeants, and Patrolmen.**

The Superintendent can discharge Patrolmen at his own pleasure; and other members of the force, with the consent of the Mayor.

In times of public peril, the Superintendent may appoint from the citizens, temporarily, any required number of **special patrolmen.**

Some members of the force are detailed to act as

detectives for the discovery of criminals. Such officers constitute a distinct department of the force.

What are a policeman's general duties?

What are the qualifications of a good policeman? Why?

What famous event happened in Chicago, on the night of May 4, 1886?

Powers of the Chief? His duties?

What are " special patrolmen? "

Chicago has cause to be proud, also, of its

FIRE DEPARTMENT.

When the fire alarm signal sounds, the firemen slide down vertical poles from their quarters above the engine room, the horses of their own accord, go instantly to their places, and, in an average time of less than a quarter of a minute after the signal is heard, the horses are hitched, the men mounted, and all are on their way toward the fire.

This Department embraces a Fire Marshal, Secretary, one or more Assistant Fire Marshals, Superintendent of City Telegraph, Fire Inspector. Veterinary Surgeon, Captains, Lieutenants, Engineers, Pipemen, Drivers, Truckmen, and Telegraph Operators.

The Fire Marshal is appointed by the Mayor, with the consent of the Council.

The Marshal appoints, with the consent of the

Mayor, all other officers and members of the Department.

He has absolute control of all such officers and members.

He has **authority to remove or destroy any building** during a fire to keep the fire from spreading, and he and his Assistant Marshals, during a fire, and for thirty-six hours afterward, have **power to arrest** suspected or disorderly persons, and to take them before a Police Magistrate for trial.

During the Great Fire of 1871. the spread of the fire on the South Side was stopped by the firemen blowing up buildings south of the fire; and great numbers of dishonest persons were arrested because they engaged in plundering buildings within the burning district.

It is the **Fire Inspector's duty,** immediately after a fire, to **investigate its cause,** find the value of the property destroyed and the amount of insurance; to find, if possible, whether the fire was caused by carelessness or by an incendiary; and to report such facts to the Fire Marshal.

The **Superintendent of City Telegraph** has charge of all the telegraph apparatus used by the Police and Fire Departments.

The duties of the other members of the Fire Department are too obvious to require explanation.

QUESTIONS.

Give an interesting fact about the Fire Department.
Powers of the Marshal? His police power?
Duties of other members of the Department?

INSPECTORS.

There are several kinds of business carried on in Chicago, which, without careful watching, would produce great damage to property, as well as disease and loss of life; and others that, resulting less harmfully, would still bring pecuniary loss to great numbers of people.

For the purpose of preventing such results, the Mayor is authorized, by ordinance, to appoint, biennially, **Inspectors of Steam Boilers, Gas Meters, Fish, Oils, and Weights and Measures.**

The **Inspector of Steam Boilers** is required to examine all steam boilers and tanks subjected to steam pressure, on request of the persons owning or using them, and to issue to each of such persons a certificate dated on the day of the examination, stating the condition of the boiler or tank.

Every **person owning or using** such boiler or tank, is required by city ordinance to ask the Inspector to make examination of the same, at least once a year, and to keep such certificate posted in a conspicuous place where the boiler or tank is used.

The **Inspector of Gas Meters**, whenever requested, examines meters furnished by a gas company to any consumer; and also ascertains the amount of gas supplied to the city by any company having a contract for such supply.

The **Inspector of Fish** has power to examine all fish and oysters found in the city, and to destroy such as are unfit for food.

The **Inspector of Oils** is required to examine oils

when requested; to find their quality, and mark the vessels containing them "Approved" or "Dangerous." All dealers in oils are required, by city ordinance to have their oils inspected before offering them for sale.

It is the duty of the **Inspector of Weights and Measures** to examine, once a year at least, all instruments used in the city for weighing and measuring; to keep a register of such examination, deliver a copy of it to the Council, and to report to the City Prosecutor, the names of all persons using incorrect weights and measures.

Persons so doing are subject to a fine of $25.00.

ELECTION COMMISSIONERS.

Elections in the City of Chicago are in charge of a **Board of Election Commissioners**, who are appointed by the County Judge, and hold office three years.

Two of the Commissioners, at least, must be selected from the two leading political parties of the State.

The Board is required, by law, to divide the city into precincts containing, as nearly as practicable, three hundred voters, and to appoint for each precinct, three Judges of Election. Two of these must be from the leading parties of the State.

The Board must appoint, also, for each precinct, two clerks of election, who must be selected from the two leading parties of the State.

QUESTIONS.

Duty of Inspector of Boilers?
Duty of persons using steam boilers?

Duties of other Inspectors?
Duties of dealers in oils?
Penalty for using false weights and measures?
State some of the duties of Election Commissioners.
Explain the reasons for such duties.

THE PUBLIC SCHOOLS.

BOARD OF EDUCATION.

The Public Schools of Chicago are under the management of the **Board of Education.** The Board consists of fifteen members, appointed by the Mayor, with the consent of the Council, and holding office for a term of three years. They receive no pay.

The Board of Education does not have **power to levy taxes** for school purposes. Neither can it buy or sell school lands, or erect school buildings, except with the consent of the Council.

But, after the Council has appropriated money for school purposes, or after the city's share of the State school fund, or any other school money, has been paid to the City Treasurer, then the **Board has absolute control** of all such funds, having power to expend them for school purposes, free from the control of the Council, except as above stated.

The Board also has power to appoint **Superintendents, Principals, Teachers,** and other employés; to divide the city into school districts; to furnish the schools with necessary supplies of all kinds; to expel unruly pupils, and to discharge inefficient teachers.

It is the duty of the Board to take entire control

of the schools; to cause candidates for Teachers to be examined; to establish rules for the government of the schools; to prescribe the course of study, and to enact ordinances necessary to carry into effect all the Board's powers and duties.

The officers of the Board are elected, annually, from the members, and are President, Vice-President, and Secretary.

The President presides at the meetings. The Secretary keeps a record of the acts of the Board, and examines and signs the pay rolls of the Teachers and other employés of the Board.

The employes of the Board, besides those above-named, are: **Supervisor of Evening Schools, Architect, Attorney, School Agent, Supply Agent, Chief Engineer, Clerk, Auditor, and Foreman of Repairs.** All employes of the Board are elected annually.

The **Superintendent** has supervision of all the public schools of the city, their equipment, apparatus and libraries, and also of Teachers and pupils.

Some of **his duties** are, to observe, teaching and discipline of the schools, and to aid Teachers with his advice, to report to the Board the names of those whose work is not satisfactory, and to keep office hours and hear requests relating to the Public Schools.

The **Assistant Superintendents** aid the Superintendent in the performance of his duties, and are subject to his direction.

Principals are required to have charge of the schools in their respective buildings, supervise the work of their Teachers, examine pupils for promotion, attend to cases requiring special discipline, and to give careful attention to the health and comfort of their pupils.

Assistants to Principals have immediate supervision of the four lowest grades of the schools.

Teachers are of two classes—Regular and Special. Special Teachers are employed to teach certain branches only, as German and music. Such Teachers are under the immediate supervision of the Superintendent of their specialty.

Each **Regular Teacher** has charge of one division of pupils. and is held responsible for the progress of such pupils in their studies.

The **Architect** is required to superintend the erection and repair of school buildings, and to see that all work upon such buildings is done properly and at a reasonable cost.

The **Attorney** attends to the legal business of the Board.

The **School Agent** has the custody of all bonds, notes, and other securities belonging to the Board; collects the rents of school lands, and the interest on such school funds as are loaned; keeps the accounts of the Board's funds, and pays the Teachers their wages, monthly.

The **Supply Agent** purchases and distributes supplies for the schools, and prepares the pay-rolls of Engineers, Janitors, Mechanics and Laborers employed by the Board.

The **Chief Engineer** visits all the school buildings to ascertain what repairs and alterations are necessary in the heating and ventilating apparatus, and superintends the making of such repairs and alterations.

The **Clerk keeps a record** of the proceedings of the Board, and **prepares pay-rolls** of Superintendents, Teachers, and other employes of the Board, except those whose pay-rolls are prepared by the Supply Agent.

The **Auditor keeps records** of all the financial transactions of the Board, and of all the funds and sources of income belonging to the Board.

It is also his **duty** to inspect all bills against the Board, and take care that none are paid, except those which are just and legal.

The **Foreman of Repairs** superintends the workmen employed in making repairs and improvements on school property, and has custody of the tools, shops and materials used in such work. It is his duty to visit every school building as often as possible, examine its condition, and recommend to the Board necessary repairs and alterations.

Besides the usual Janitor's duties, **Janitors of the Chicago schools are required to display the National flag** belonging to each school building, on the building on all legal holidays, and during the morning session of school on every Monday of the school year.

ELECTION OF SCHOOL BOARD EMPLOYES.

Superintendents, Teachers, Engineers and Janitors are elected by the Board annually, at the first regular meeting after the close of the summer term.

All Principals and Teachers not charged with unsatisfactory work during the year, are together declared elected by the Board;—an example of "Civil Service Reform" worthy of imitation in all branches of government.

Superintendents and Assistant Superintendents are elected by ballot.

SALARIES.

As soon as possible after January 1, every year, the City Council appropriates such sum as it deems proper for one year, for the use of the Board of Education; and as soon as possible after such appropriation, the Board fixes the salaries of all its employes for the current year.

TEXT BOOKS.

Text books in use in the Schools can be changed only at or before the last regular meeting of the Board in June of each year. Changes in the course of instruction can be made only in the same manner.

EVENING SCHOOLS.

Evening Schools are supported by a special appropriation made annually by the City Council. They are under the general control of the Board, and the immediate care of the **Supervisor of Evening Schools.**

They open on the first Monday evening of October, and continue till the Board decides to close them.

OTHER SCHOOLS.

The Board also supports a Manual Training School, and Schools for Deaf Mutes.

COMPULSORY EDUCATION.

The State law requires that every child between the ages of seven and fourteen years, shall attend school at least sixteen weeks each year, beginning at the opening of the school year. Parents and others having control of a child, are liable to a fine of from three to twenty dollars, if they prevent such attendance. In pursuance of this law, the Chicago Board appoints **Truant Officers,** to see that this law is enforced. It is the duty of these officers to arrest truants and deliver them to their Teachers, and to **prosecute parents** and others who violate the law.

QUESTIONS.

How is the Board of Education appointed? How many members has it? How is it organized?

What power, if any, has the Board in regard to taxation.

How is its use of school funds limited?

In what respects is it independent of control in its use of such funds?

What are some of its powers and duties in regard to the general control and management of the schools?

Duties of the Superintendent of Schools?

Duties of Assistant Superintendents, Principals, and Assistants to Principals?

Classes of Teachers?

Duties of Architect, School Agent, Supply Agent, Chief Engineer, Clerk, Auditor, and Foreman of Repairs?

Janitor's duty in respect to flag?

When can Text Books be changed?

Give substance of Compulsory Education Law.

Under certain rules and regulations, the pupils of the City Schools are allowed to draw books from

THE PUBLIC LIBRARY.

The laws of the State of Illinois authorize any incorporated Town, Village or Township, to establish a free Public Library; and any incorporated city, to establish both such a library and also a free reading room, and to levy a tax for the support of the same.

In cities of 100,000 or 'more inhabitants, the tax can not exceed one-half mill on the dollar annually, on all the taxable property of the city; in other cities, one mill; and in towns, villages and townships, two mills.

In pursuance of this law, Chicago has established a Library and Reading Room, to which, under certain necessary rules, all the residents of the city have access.

The Public Library and Reading Room are managed by a **Board of nine Directors,** who are appointed by the Mayor, with the consent of the Council, for a term of three years.   They receive no pay.

The money belonging to the Library Fund is kept on deposit with the City Treasurer, but the Directors control its expenditure.

The Directors appoint a Librarian and Assistants,

fix their pay, and make rules relating to the use of the books and Reading Room.

The Library contains 154,000 books.

CHICAGO PARKS

The greater **Parks** of Chicago, **Lincoln, Garfield, Douglas, Humboldt,** and the **South Parks,** and the **Boulevards** respectively connected with them, are governed by three Boards of Park Commissioners.

The members of the North and West Park Boards are appointed by the Governor of the State, with the consent of the Senate, and those of the South Park Board, by the Judges of the Circuit Court of Cook County. Their term of office is five years, and they receive no pay.

Each of such Boards has power to acquire lands for Parks, by purchase or by condemnation proceedings, that is, by suit in a court, and to levy a tax for Park purposes on all the land within its Park District.

Park Boards also have power, for the purpose of connecting a Park with any portion of the city, to take control of and improve any street lying in the Park District, provided consent in writing is given by the owners of a majority of the front feet on such street, and provided the Council concurs by the passage of a suitable ordinance. A street so taken is called a Boulevard.

For the purpose of paying the expenses of above improvement, a Park Board may levy taxes on property contiguous to such improvement, and may borrow money for general Park and Boulevard purposes, issuing bonds therefor to an amount not exceeding one mill on the dollar of taxable property within the Park District.

CHICAGO SANITARY DISTRICT.

The object of the law creating this District is to provide a channel for water in which the sewage of Chicago may be conducted away from Lake Michigan.

This is necessary, because sewage flowing into the Lake is carried out beyond the Crib of the Waterworks, thus rendering the city's water unfit for use.

The District was established in the year 1889, by a vote of the people within its territory, held in pursuance of a law of the State, which went into effect July 1, 1889.

The District embraces all of the city, except the part south of Eighty-seventh street; also contiguous territory three to four miles wide lying west of and adjoining the city, as well as a portion of Lake Michigan wide enough to include the Crib of the Waterworks.   .

The affairs of the District are managed by a Board of nine Trustees, who are elected by the voters of the District, and hold office five years.

The Board has power to create and maintain one or more drainage channels in the District, and, if such channels extend beyond the District, the Board's powers extend with it.

The Board may levy taxes on property within the District, and may borrow money and acquire property for District purposes by purchase or condemnation proceedings.

The law requires that any channel of the District, into which sewage is to be discharged, must be so made that its water will flow at the rate of 200 cubic feet per minute for each 1,000 persons residing in the District.

It is a well-known fact that water in motion has a tendency to purify itself. And it has been found that a stream of water, flowing at the rate, and being of a volume which has the ratio to population, above given, will purify itself of all corrupt matter contained in the sewage of such a population, and will, therefore, not be injurious to people living near its channel.

QUESTIONS.

What is the law for the support of Public Libraries and Reading Rooms?

How is the Chicago Library Board constituted?

Duties of its members?

Number of books in the Library?

Name the principal Parks and Boulevards of Chicago.

Who have control of these?

Powers and duties of the Park Commissioners?

What is the Sanitary District?

How are its affairs managed?

Explain how a channel of water receiving sewage can be kept pure.

COOK COUNTY.

The **territory first organized as Cook County** included what are now the counties of Cook, DuPage, Lake, McHenry, Will, and Iroquois. The **organization** occurred on **March 4, 1831.**

The Legislature created Iroquois a separate county on February 26, 1833; Will, on January 12, 1836; McHenry, on January 16, 1836; DuPage, on February 9, 1839; and Lake, on March 9, 1839.

When the **State Constitution of 1870** was adopted, **Cook County** was under township organization, but that constitution provided a government for Cook different from that of other counties under such organization.

Under that constitution, and the laws made to carry it into effect, the governing body of the county is given large and varied powers similar to those enjoyed by the Chicago City Council.

It has both legislative and executive power, and retains and pays many employés unknown to the other counties of the State. It is commonly known as

THE COUNTY BOARD.

It consists of fifteen Commissioners chosen annually; ten elected from the City of Chicago and five from the towns of the county outside of the city.

Under a law enacted in 1887, a **President of the Board** is elected by the people. Each voter can designate on his ballot the candidate for commissioner whom he wishes to be President. The candidate who receives the highest number of such votes, becomes President of the Board.

It is the **duty of the Board to provide** for all the **expenses** of the county for which the general laws of the State make no provision.

Within the first quarter of the year, therefore, the Board must pass an appropriation bill for all such expenses of the current year; and it has no power to pass an additional appropriation bill, or incur any additional expense during the year.

The Board **can not let, privately, any contracts** for supplies, material, or work, for county purposes. **Bids must be advertised for** in some newspaper published in the county, and contracts must be let to the lowest responsible bidder.

All work for the county must be done under contracts thus made, except **in cases of emergency,** when the Superintendent of Public Service may purchase supplies amounting to not more than $500.00.

All contracts must be approved by the Board, and signed by its **President, the Comptroller, and the Superintendent of Public Service.**

PRESIDENT OF THE BOARD.

The **President has powers and duties** similar to those of the mayor of a city.

He is required to preside at the meetings of the Board, and to personally inspect all the accounts of the Superintendent of Public Service and the County

Comptroller, and report to the Board if he finds such accounts incorrect.

He can not submit to the Board any **proposition to spend money,** unless such proposition is in writing signed by the Commissioner offering it.

He can **veto appropriations** of money by the Board; and such appropriations can not be passed except by a majority of at least four-fifths of the members of the Board.

EMPLOYÈS OF THE COUNTY BOARD.

The principal employès of the County Board are: **County Attorney and his Assistant, Superintendent of Public Service, Clerk of the Board, Committee Clerk, Warden of County Hospital, Medical Superintendent of Insane Asylum, Medical Superintendent of Poor House, County Physician, County Agent, Chief Jury Clerk, Engineers of County Buildings, Surveyor, Electrician, and Farmer.**

All such employés, except Clerk of the Board and Jury Clerk, are elected, and their pay is fixed, by the Board, for a term of one year.

It is the **duty of the County Attorney** to appear for the county in all suits where it is a party; to furnish the Board with legal opinions on all questions submitted to him by it; and to attend to all the legal business of the county for which the Board is responsible.

The **Superintendent of Public Service has charge of the purchase and distribution** of all supplies which are used in the departments of the county government and the institutions of the county which are under the exclusive care of the County Board.

The Clerk of the Board is appointed by the County Clerk.

He attends the meetings of the Board, and keeps a record of its proceedings.

He is ex-officio County Comptroller, and, as such, performs for the county, duties similar to those of the Comptroller of the city of Chicago. [See page 31.]

The Committee Clerk keeps a record of all committee meetings.

The Chief Jury Clerk furnishes to the County Clerk the names of persons capable of serving as petit jurors. He is required, by law, to name only persons of intelligence and good character for such service.

From the lists thus made out, the County Clerk furnishes names to the Sheriff, whose duty it is to summon persons to serve as jurors.

The County Electrician has charge of the dynamos and all other electrical apparatus owned by the county.

QUESTIONS.

When was Cook County organized?

What territory did it first include?

Describe its County Board.

What general powers has the Board?

How is its President elected?

What is the Board's duty in regard to the annual appropriation?

How must contracts for supplies be let?

What are the President's duties?

Name the principal employés of the Board, and state the principal duties of each.

How are they appointed?

THE COUNTY CHARITABLE INSTITUTIONS.

In the town of Jefferson, at the railway station Dunning, Cook County owns a farm called the **County Poor Farm.** On it are located the **County Poor House, Insane Asylum,** and buildings for the use of the **County Farmer.**

The **Farmer** resides on the Farm, and **superintends its cultivation.** Inmates of the Poor House and Insane Asylum, if able to work, are employed by the Farmer. The products of the Farm are used by such County Institutions as need them.

The **Hospital of Cook County** is located in Chicago at the southwest corner of South Wood and West Harrison streets.

The **Warden of the Hospital** and the **Superintendents of the Poor House and Insane Asylum,** are required to reside in their respective Institutions; to employ kind and skillful assistants; to see that the inmates receive all necessary attention, and to incur no unnecessary expense.

The **County Physician** admits persons to the Poor House, has charge of the Detention Hospital for the Insane (which is in the County Jail building), has oversight of the health of inmates of the County Jail, and supervises the transfer of patients from the Hospital to the Poor House.

The **County Agent also has authority** to order that persons be admitted to the Poor House, to the Hospital, and to the Detention Hospital for the Insane, if he finds, on inquiry, that such persons have no relatives in the county who should provide for them.

It is **his especial duty** to relieve those persons suffering actual want outside of the County Institutions. But, to be entitled to such relief, persons applying for it must prove that they have lived in the county at least six months before becoming dependent.

The **Engineers** of the different **County Buildings** have the care of the heating apparatus of the same; and, at the Poor House and Insane Asylum, they have also charge of the water systems, and keep the hose and pipes ready for instant use in case of fire.

It is the **duty of the County Surveyor** to survey, that is, learn the boundaries and location of any piece of land, whenever requested, and furnish to the person requesting, a copy of the surveyor's record, and a plat, viz., a map of the land surveyed.

THE COUNTY NORMAL SCHOOL.

This Institution is located at Normal Park, and is supported by the County Board for the **purpose of training teachers** for the public schools of the county not within the city of Chicago.

It is under the control of the

COUNTY BOARD OF EDUCATION,

Which consists of seven members, elected by the Commissioners, and holding office during a term of two years.   The County Superintendent of Schools is, ex-officio, also a member of this Board.

The **County Board of Education** sustains about the same relation to the County Commissioners and the Normal School, as the Chicago Board sustains to the Council and City Schools.

The Commissioners appropriate, annually, a sum of money for the support of the Normal School, and the Board hires a Principal and Teachers, and other necessary employés for the school, furnishes it with supplies, and supervises its work.

All the officers above named, except Surveyor and County Farmer, are peculiar to Cook County.

In addition, Cook has all the officers that any other county in the State has (and a few others), viz.:

Judges of the Superior,* Circuit, County and Probate Courts; Sheriff, Treasurer, Recorder, County Clerk; Clerks of the Superior,* Circuit, Probate, Criminal* and Appellate Courts; Coroner, State's Attorney and Superintendent of Schools.

QUESTIONS.

Name the County Charitable Institutions.

Where are they located?

What is the object of each?

What is the object of the County Normal School?

Under whose care is it?

---

* Officers of Cook County only.

COURTS IN COOK COUNTY.

Cook County constitutes one judicial circuit. The work of this circuit is done by the Circuit, Superior and Criminal Courts.

The Criminal Court is presided over, in turn, by Judges of the Circuit and Superior Courts. ·

It has original and exclusive jurisdiction* in all criminal cases where the offense is committed against the laws of the State.

It has appellate jurisdiction in criminal cases appealed from Justices of the Peace.

The Circuit and Superior Courts have original jurisdiction in all civil disputes, for which, remedy is provided by the laws of the State.

They have appellate jurisdiction in civil cases appealed from Justices of the Peace.

Their Judges are elected for equal terms, six years, and are paid equal salaries.

There are several Judges of each of these courts, and their number may be increased from time to time, by act of the Legislature, as the population of the county increases.

The county has, also, a County Court and a Probate Court.

The former has exclusive jurisdiction in suits for the collection of taxes, and in trying persons supposed to be insane.

It has concurrent jurisdiction with the Circuit and Superior Courts in civil disputes involving not more

* For definitions, see pages 90 and 91.

than $1,000, and in cases appealed from Justices of the Peace.*

The **Probate Court** has original and exclusive **jurisdiction in matters relating to wills, the settlement of estates** of deceased persons, **apprentices, guardians of minors, and conservators of the insane and imbecile.**

The last two Courts have but one Judge each. The term of such Judges is four years.

Cook County constitutes the **First District of the Appellate Court.**

The Judges of this court, three in number, are assigned to it by the Supreme Court, from the Superior, or the Circuit Court Judges from this or other circuits.

All the above courts are called "Courts of Record."

Nearly all kinds of cases, except criminal cases called "felonies," if appealed from courts of record, must first be taken to an Appellate Court.

In all cases where less than $1,000 is in dispute, such court's decision is final, unless the court itself elects to send the case to the Supreme Court on account of some new or peculiar question involved.†

DUTIES OF COOK COUNTY OFFICERS.

The **duties** of the officers of Cook County are the same as those of like officers in other counties of the State.

SHERIFF.

The **Sheriff's principal duties** are : **to attend the sessions** of all the above **courts,** preserving order in

---

* For "Concurrent Jurisdiction." see page 9.

† For jurisdiction of Supreme Court, see page 113.

them, and executing the commands of the Judges; to **serve summonses, writs,** and other judicial papers; to prevent disorderly conduct wherever he is, and to **arrest offenders** against the law.

He has **custody of the Court House and Jail,** takes convicted prisoners to the Penitentiary and House of of Correction, and hangs criminals condemned to death.

As Cook County has nearly twenty courts in session ten months every year, it is plain that the Sheriff can not himself attend all of them, to say nothing of performing the countless other duties of his office. Hence, he is authorized to employ a fixed number of deputies, bailiffs and clerks to assist him. The deputies have the same authority as the Sheriff himself to serve writs and other legal papers.

TREASURER.

It is his duty to receive and care for all money paid for Town, City, County and State taxes, and to pay it out only on the order of the County Board, or in the manner specially provided by law.

To keep books of his accounts as Treasurer, and have them always open to the inspection of the public.

To report to the County Board, at each of its regular sessions, all sums of money paid out by him.

RECORDER.

It is his duty to provide his office with suitable books, and, on request, to **copy** in them, **deeds, mortgages,** and other papers relating to interest in real estate; also, chattel mortgages. This is called **recording deeds,** etc.

Before recording such documents, the Recorder places on the back of each, a certificate signed by himself stating the day, hour and minute when it was received for recording.

The Recorder of Cook County also furnishes **abstracts of title.**

An abstract of title is a history of everything that has been done affecting the title, or right, to the piece of real estate under examination.

COUNTY CLERK.

It is the **duty of the County Clerk** to keep a record of the acts of the County Court, of the County Board, and of all orders for money drawn on the County Treasurer.

To issue marriage licenses.

To compute the Town, County, City and State Tax of every person owning property in Cook County, enter it in proper books, and issue these to the appropriate collectors.*

The County Clerk of Cook County is also, **ex-officio, County Comptroller.**

In the latter capacity, it is his duty to audit the accounts of the County Board, to see that the county suffers no pecuniary loss.

He submits to the Board, annually, an estimate of the probable expenses of the county government for the next year.

The **duties of Comptroller** are, in fact, performed by the County Clerk's deputy, the Clerk of the Board of Commissioners.

* See page 92; topic, "County Clerk."

CIRCUIT CLERK.

Some of his duties are to receive and file papers in suits begun in the Circuit Court.

To issue writs, summonses, and other legal papers to the Sheriff to execute.

To keep records of the acts of the court.

To furnish copies of such records, on request.

To keep account of the costs of legal proceedings, and to issue to the Sheriff writs to collect such costs from the persons liable to pay them.

The Clerks of the Superior, Probate, County, Criminal and Appellate Courts perform similar duties for their courts.

All the above Clerks have power to appoint deputies, for whose acts the respective Clerks are held responsible.

CORONER.

He examines, with the aid of a jury, the body of any person killed by accident, or having died from any mysterious cause, calls witnesses of the event, if there are any, and ascertains the cause of death, if possible, reporting such examination to the County Clerk.

He may cause the arrest of any person suspected of killing the deceased, and commit him to the Grand Jury.

It is the Coroner's duty to act as Sheriff, if the Sheriff's office becomes vacant, or if the Sheriff is interested in a suit.

STATE'S ATTORNEY.

The State's Attorney's chief duties are to aid the Grand Jury in the investigation of criminal matters, to draw indictments,* and to conduct trials in the Criminal Court.

SUPERINTENDENT OF SCHOOLS.

This officer is required to **visit the schools** of the county outside of the City of Chicago, notice the teachers' methods, the branches taught, text books used, and the general condition of the schools.

To **instruct teachers** in the best methods of teaching.

To **hold county teachers' institutes.**

To **examine candidates for teachers,** and issue licenses only to those capable of teaching skillfully.

To decide contests in reference to school law.

To **divide the money** received from the State, **among the townships** of the county, in proportion to the children under twenty-one years of age in the respective townships.

To **examine and approve the bonds, books and accounts** of township school treasurers before issuing money to them.

To **remove from office, directors** of school districts who do not perform their duties properly, and to cause elections to be held to fill such vacancies.

To report to the State Superintendent whatever facts the latter needs for his report to the Governor.

All of the above officers may appoint deputies or assistants.

The County Board fixes the pay of both officers and

* See page 89.

assistants, except, in a few instances, where the compensation is determined by State law.

QUESTIONS.

Name the Courts of Record in Cook County.

What is meant by the "jurisdiction" of a court?

Define the kinds of jurisdiction.

What jurisdiction has each of the courts of Cook County?

What kind of cases may be appealed from the Appellate to the Superior Court?

What officers has Cook County in common with the other counties of the State?

State some of the most important duties of such officers.

What is an "abstract of title?"

Having finished our study of the State's two most important sub-divisions, its greatest City and County, we will now pass to an examination of its other parts, and of the State at large.

In making such examination, we will take up the political units of the State in the order of their size, beginning with the least.

THE SCHOOL DISTRICT.*

Q. What are the officers of a school district called?

A. Directors.

Q. How many directors are there in each district?

A. Three.

Q. For what term are they elected?

A. Three years.

Q. When are they elected?

A. One director is elected every year at the annual district election, which is held on the third Saturday of April. Women may be directors. Directors must be 21 years old, and able to read and write the English language.

Q. What notice must be given before the election?

A. Ten days before the election the directors must put up notices in three of the most public places in the district, stating the place where the election will be held, when the voting will begin and end, and the questions that will be voted on.

Q. What must the directors do within ten days after the election?

A. They must meet and choose one of their number president and another clerk of the board of directors.

Q. What are the president's duties?

A. To preside at the meetings and execute the orders of the board.

Q. What are the clerk's duties?

A. To keep a record of the acts of the board, and submit it on the first Mondays of April and October to the town treasurer. On or before July 7, annually, to

* Cook County has school district government like the other counties of the State, and town government like the counties which are under township organization.

70

report to the town treasurer such facts as the treasurer must report to the county superintendent.

DUTIES OF DIRECTORS.

Q. What are the duties of the whole board of directors?

AS TO TEACHERS?

A. To appoint teachers and fix their pay, and to dismiss them for incompetency or bad conduct.

• AS TO SCHOOL MANAGEMENT?

A. To visit schools and make rules for their government. To direct what branches shall be taught. Not to permit a change of text books oftener than once in four years.

AS TO REPORTS TO TREASURER?

A. To report to the town treasurer whatever facts the law requires him to report to the county superintendent.

AS TO TAXATION?

A. To levy a tax sufficient, with the district's share of the State fund, to maintain school at least five and not more than nine months in the year, and to erect necessary school-buildings.

Directors can not levy a tax of more than three per cent. for building and two per cent. for other educational purposes. They can levy a tax sufficient to maintain school nine months of the year, if the tax does not exceed two per cent. of the assessed value of all the property in the district.

AS TO REPORTS TO VOTERS?

A. Directors must at the annual district election submit to the voters a report of all sums of money received and paid out by them during the year (having sent a copy to the township treasurer within five days of the time of election), and must post on the door of house where the election is held the township treasurer's exhibit of the sums received and expended by the district during the preceding year. They must also give the names of all persons between the ages of twelve and twenty-one in the district who can not read and write, and state the causes of the neglect to educate them.

AS TO COMPULSORY EDUCATION.

To compel all children between the ages of eight and fourteen years, to attend school, at least twelve weeks in each school year. Failure to perform this duty subjects directors to prosecution and a fine of ten dollars.

HOW DISTRICTS RECEIVE THEIR SHARE OF THE STATE FUND.

Q. How do districts receive their share of the State school tax ? *

A. On the first Monday in January every year, next after taking the census of the State, the State auditor issues to the superintendent of schools in each county an order on the county treasurer for a sum of money proportioned to the number of children in the county under twenty-one years of age.

Next, the county superintendent must require each township treasurer to give a sufficient bond for the safe-keeping of the money to be paid over to him, and then pay to him a sum proportioned to the children under twenty-one in his town.†

The trustees then find how much each district is entitled to, the sum being proportioned to the children in the district under twenty-one. They then let the directors of each district know what sum belongs to their district, and that sum is paid out by the township treasurer as the directors give orders.‡ The directors' orders for the payment of money must be in writing.

* In addition to the State tax, each district receives also its proportionate share of the following funds ; viz : Interest on the state, county and township school funds, and the fines and forfeitures collected by justices of the peace.

† The county superintendent must not pay this sum unless the directors have made their annual reports according to law.

‡ The treasurer should withhold all money until the directors have returned to him their schedules; which they should return in April and October.

HOW DISTRICTS MAY BE DIVIDED.

Q. Who lay out townships in school districts?

A. The trustees.

Q. How can the boundaries of districts be altered?

A. The trustees may alter them when petitioned so to do either by a majority of the voters of the district or districts affected, or by two-thirds of the voters of the territory involved. Within ten days from final action upon a petition by trustees, an appeal may be taken from such action to the county superintendent. The county superintendent may grant or refuse the petition on appeal.*

TRANSFERRING PUPILS.

Q. How may pupils be transferred from one district to another?

A. By getting the written consent of a majority of the directors of both districts.

II. THE TOWN.

TOWNS AND TOWNSHIPS DISTINGUISHED.

Q. In what town (or township) do you live? Give its bounds. What cities or villages does it contain? How many are its school districts?

Q. Who lay out towns?

A. Three commissioners, appointed by the county board. (See page 22.)

Q. Who lay out townships?

A. United States surveyors, when the Government lands are first surveyed. A township is six miles square.

Q. Do the "towns" of a county coincide with its "townships?"

* See Sec. 33 of School Laws.

A. Not always. But it is the duty of county boards to so lay out towns that they will coincide with townships, if possible.

Q. What is the chief difference between "towns" and "townships."

A. Towns govern themselves in all local matters. Townships govern themselves in school affairs only. In all other local matters they are governed by the county boards.

Q. What is the origin of "town government" in Illinois?

A. In 1848 a new State constitution was adopted, which provided that town government might be organized in all counties where a majority of the people voted for it. The constitution adopted in 1870 contains a similar provision.

Q. Have all the counties in the State accepted town government, or "township organization," as it is more commonly called?

A. No. About twenty counties have not yet done so. These counties are in the southern part of the State.

Q. Has the county in which you live adopted township organization? If yes, when did it do so?

TOWN OFFICERS—THEIR TERMS OF OFFICE.

Q. What officers do towns have, and what are their terms of office?

A. One or more supervisors, term, two years. A collector, a clerk, an assessor; term of each, one year. Three highway commissioners; term three years, one commissioner being elected annually. Two or more justices of the peace; two or more constables; term of each, four years. One or more poundmasters may be elected at

town meetings, to serve one year.* A commissioner of
Canada thistles may be appointed by the board or town
auditors, to serve three years. If such commissioner is
not so appointed, the county board must appoint one, if
petitioned by twenty-five land owners in the town to be
affected, or in the towns adjoining, the same.

Q. In what case has a town more than one supervisor?

A. In towns of 4,000 inhabitants there is one assistant, and for every 2,500 above 4,000 one supervisor is
added.

Q. In what case are there more than two justices and
two constables?

A. One justice and one constable are added for every
1,000 inhabitants above 2,000 till there are five of each.

TOWN MEETING.

Q. What do towns have that unorganized townships lack?

A. Town meetings.

Q. What is a town meeting?

A. It is a meeting of the voters of the town to elect
town officers, adopt rules for the government of the
town, and to hear the reports of the town officers for
the preceding year.

Q. When is the annual town meeting held?

A. On the first Tuesday of April.

Q. What must precede the meeting?

A. The town clerk must post notices of the time and
place of holding the meeting in three of the most public
places in the town ten days before the meeting, and in-
sert the notice also in a newspaper, if any is published
in the town.

ORGANIZATION OF THE TOWN MEETING.

Q. How does a town meeting prepare for business?

A. Between 8 and 9 o'clock the town clerk calls the

* In towns coincident with townships one school trustee is elected annually at
town meeting. See page 21. For election of school treasurer, see page 21.

meeting to order, and calls on the voters present to elect one of their number moderator.

Q. What must the moderator do before assuming his office?

A. He must take an oath, faithfully to discharge his duties.

Q. What are his duties?

A. To act as a judge of election and preside over the meeting during the transaction of miscellaneous business.

Q. What further duties has the clerk after the election of moderator?

A. He must write all the proceedings of the meeting in a book known as the "town records," and must sign his name to the record of each meeting. The moderator must also sign his name to the same.

Q. After the moderator is chosen and has taken his oath of office, what is next done?

A. The ballot box is produced and voting for town officers begins.

Q. How are town officers voted for?

A. By ballot. That is, each voter hands a ticket containing the names of the candidates for whom he wishes to vote to a judge of election, who puts it in the ballot box.

Q. Who besides the moderator are judges of election?

A. The supervisor, collector and assessor.

Q. What are the duties of judges of election?

A. To receive the ballots (or tickets), not permit any unqualified person to vote, and to count the votes after the polls are closed.

Q. What persons have a right to vote?

A. All men 21 years old or older, who are citizens of

the United States, and have lived in the State one year, in the county ninety days, and in the voting precinct thirty days next preceding the election.

When towns have more than 450 voters, it is the duty of the county board to provide two or more voting places, to appoint three judges for each, and to direct that the general business of the town shall be done at one of said places.

POWERS AND DUTIES OF TOWN MEETINGS.

Q. What besides electing officers is done at town meeting ?

A. Miscellaneous business is attended to.

Q. When is this done ?

A. At 2 o'clock in the afternoon the ballot box is closed, and the moderator calls the meeting to order for miscellaneous business.

Q. What are some of the things that may be done under the name of miscellaneous business ?

A. Under the name of miscellaneous business the voters may hear and act upon the reports of officers for the preceding year. May order the raising of money by taxation for roads, bridges, and some other objects. May direct the proper officers to commence and defend law-suits for the town. May offer rewards for the destruction of Canada thistles. May offer rewards for planting trees by public roads. May make rules about fences in the town. May regulate or forbid the running at large of stock. May provide for public wells and watering places. May forbid the doing of anything that will lessen the healthfulness of the town. May decide whether the road tax shall be paid in money or in work. May provide for fining any one who shall break any of the rules adopted at town meeting. No fine can be more than $50.00.

Q. How may votes be taken on questions of miscellaneous business?

A. In three ways. *Viva voce*, that is, by answering "Aye" or "No" to the questions put to the meeting by the moderator; by division of the house, that is, by those favoring a motion, moving to one side of the house, those opposing, to the other; and by standing to be counted.

Q. What follows miscellaneous business?

A. After the moderator announces that it is closed, the ballot box is again produced, and voting for town officers begins again and continues until the closing of the polls. As soon as the polls are closed, the judges of election count the votes, and the clerk makes a record of the result and reads this publicly to the meeting.

Q. If a town office becomes vacant by death, resignation or other means, what is done?

A. The town board of appointment, consisting of the supervisor, clerk and justices of the peace, choose some person to fill the vacancy during the remainder of the term.

OATH AND BONDS OF TOWN OFFICERS.

Q. What must all town officers do before taking possession of their offices?

A. They must take an oath in which they promise to support the constitution of the United States and of Illinois, and to faithfully perform the duties of their offices.

Every officer that has public money to handle must give an official bond for double the sum of money that he will receive, to secure the public against loss.

Q. What is an official bond?

A. It is a written promise by an officer and at least

two other persons to pay into the public treasury a certain sum of money if the officer does not take proper care of the public money that may come into his hands.

TOWN BOARDS.

Q. Name the various town boards, and state who compose them and what their duties are?

A. *The board of appointment* has been already described.

The board of health consists of the supervisors, the assessor and town clerk. It is their duty to prevent the spread of contagious diseases.

The board of auditors consists of the supervisor, clerk, and one or more justices of the peace. It is their duty to examine all claims against the town, and to see that the town is not defrauded out of any money. For this purpose they meet at the town clerk's office twice a year, on the Tuesday before the annual meeting of the county board, and on the Tuesday before the annual town meeting.

At these meetings the accounts of all the town officers are examined for the purpose of learning whether the public money has been properly cared for and judiciously expended.

The board of equalization consists of the assessor, clerk and supervisor. This board meets on the fourth Monday in June, every year, to equalize assessments of the value of property. The assessor may set too high a value on some property and too low a value on other property. The owners of the former would pay too much tax, the owners of the latter too little. It is the duty of the board to equalize all the assessor's valuations as nearly as possible.

DUTIES OF TOWN OFFICERS.

SUPERVISORS.

Q. What are the duties of the principal supervisor?

A. To act as treasurer of all town money except the school and the highway and bridge funds.

To oversee the town paupers.

To attend meetings of the county board.

To report to the town board of auditors one week before the annual town meeting all sums of money received and paid out by him during the year.

To file with the town clerk, one week before the annual town meeting, a statement showing what sums of money are due the town and what sums the town owes. (This statement the clerk must copy into the town records and read at the town meeting.)

To carry on lawsuits for the recovery of fines and penalties due the town.

Q. What are the duties of assistant supervisors.

A. They have no authority in town affairs (except as members of the board of health), but in the county board they have the same powers as the principal supervisor.

CLERK.

Q. What are the clerk's duties?

A. To take care of all records, books and papers belonging to the town.

To record all acts of town meetings and of the town board of auditors.

To send to the county clerk, on or before the second Tuesday in August, a statement of the amount of taxes to be levied in his town for that year.

ASSESSOR, COLLECTOR.

Q. What is the assessor's duty?

A. To make an assessment of all the property in the town.

Q. What is an assessment?

A. It is a value set on property and written down in the assessor's book for the purpose of taxation.

Q. How is each man's tax found?

A. By multiplying the value of his property as fixed by the assessor by the rate per cent. of taxation.

Q. What are the collector's duties?

A. To collect the town taxes. To pay those levied for school purposes to the treasurer of the school fund ; those levied for roads and bridges, to the treasurer of the highway commissioners ; and those levied for general town purposes, to the principal supervisor.

SCHOOL TRUSTEES.

Q. What are the duties of trustees of schools?

A. To divide the township into school districts according to the wishes of a majority of the people.

To divide the school money among the districts in proportion to the number of children in each, under twenty-one years of age.

To withhold money from all districts that do not keep their schools according to law, and in obedience to the directions of the county and State superintendents.

To control township high schools, when such have been established.

To appoint a treasurer of the school funds.

SCHOOL TREASURER.

Q. What are the school treasurer's duties?

A. To take care of the school money of the township.

To keep the permanent school funds at interest.

To report annually to the trustees, all sums received, paid out, and in hand.

To settle twice a year with the directors, making a sworn statement that will show the amount each district is entitled to.

To report under oath, on or before September 30, annually, to the county superintendent the condition of the township funds.

To report to the county superintendent such facts as are called for by the State superintendent.

HIGHWAY COMMISSIONERS.

Q. What are the duties of highway commissioners?

A. To choose one of their number treasurer.

To divide the town into a suitable number of road districts.

To lay out new roads and alter old ones, and to build new bridges, when they deem such acts necessary.

To keep roads and bridges in repair.

To put up guide boards at forks and crossings.

To levy a road tax and see that it is collected, or an equivalent amount of work done on the roads of the town.

To appoint, in towns where road tax is paid in labor, an overseer of highways in each road district.

To give directions to overseers of highways about the work in their respective road districts.

OVERSEERS OF HIGHWAYS.

Q. What is the duty of overseers of highways?

A. To superintend the road work done in their respective districts.

2

POUNDMASTER AND COMMISSIONER OF CANADA THISTLES.

Q. What is the poundmaster's duty?

A. To shut up stock found running at large, and hold it till the owners take charge of it.

Q What is the duty of the commissioner of Canada thistles?

A. To destroy all Canada thistles found growing in the town.

JUSTICES AND CONSTABLES

Q. What are the duties of justices of the peace?

A. To try civil causes when the sum in dispute is not more than $200.

To try criminal causes, when the punishment is by fine only and the fine is not more than $200.

To try offenders in cases of assault and battery, and in some other cases.

To examine those accused of offenses punishable by imprisonment in the county jail or penitentiary, and if the evidence shows their guilt, to hold them to bail or send them to jail, to remain till the meeting of the grand jury.

Q. What are the duties of constables?

A. To stop all disorderly conduct that they witness, and to execute the orders of justices of the peace and other magistrates.

CIVIL CAUSES.

Q. What is a civil cause?

A. It is a suit in court to compel the defendant to pay the plaintiff a sum of money for a debt due or an injury done to the plaintiff, or to recover possession of property.

CRIMINAL CAUSES.

Q. What is a criminal cause?

A. It is a suit brought to secure the punishment of some person who has offended against a public law.

Q. What is a fine?

A. It is a sum of money to be paid into the public treasury by an offender against law as a punishment for his offense.

Q. What is an assault?

A. An attempt by one person to strike another. If the act is done, the offense becomes assault and battery.

HOLDING TO BAIL.

Q. What is " holding to bail?"

A. It is compelling a prisoner to produce a certain number of persons who will promise in writing to pay into the public treasury a given sum of money, if the prisoner, being set at liberty, does not afterward appear in court on a certain day.

PAY OF TOWN OFFICERS.

Q. What can you say of the pay of town officers?

A. Some are paid by the day, others partly by the day and partly in fees. Those paid by the day receive from $1.25 to $2.50 per day. The fees vary widely in amount, and are fixed by State law.

Q. What is a fee?

A. A certain sum to be received for a certain service. For example, the clerk receives twenty-five cents for posting a notice of a town meeting.

SPECIAL TOWN MEETINGS.

Q. Can there be more than one town meeting in the same year?

A. Special town meetings may be held when the supervisor, clerk, and a justice of the peace, or any two of these officers, together with at least fifteen voters, sign a written statement that a special town meeting is necessary, and file this statement in the town clerk's office. This statement must describe the object of the meeting.

Notice must then be given as for other town meetings, the notice stating the object for which the meeting is called. No business can be done at a special town meeting, except such as is described in the statement filed with the clerk and contained in the clerk's notice of the meeting.

THE NATURE OF TOWN GOVERNMENT.

Q. What three kinds of acts are done in governing a town?

A. Legislative, executive and judicial.

Q. Who do the first?

A. The voters at town meeting, when they vote on motions during the transaction of miscellaneous business. The motions that they adopt become laws for the government of the town.

Q. Who do the second?

A. The supervisor, school trustees and highway commissioners. They see that the laws made at town meeting (and also State laws) are put into effect, or executed.

Q. Who perform the third kind of acts?

A. Justices of the peace and constables. They enforce obedience to the laws by punishing those who break them.

As in the town, so in the village, the city, the county, the State, and the United States, we shall find these three departments of government, and only these, namely ; the legislative or law-making, the executive, or that which puts the law into operation, and the judicial, or law-enforcing.

Q. What kind of a government is that of a town?

A. A pure democracy. The people themselves make the laws.

Q. What kind of a government is that of an unorganized township?

A. A representative democracy. The local laws for the township (except in school matters) are made by representatives chosen by the people; namely, the county commissioners.

(It is to be remembered that over the laws made as above described, are the general laws made by the State legislature for towns and townships alike.)

OFFICERS OF TOWNSHIPS.

Q. What officers do townships have?

A. They have three school trustees, one trustee being elected on the second Saturday in April each year; and a school treasurer, elected biennially by the trustees.

In counties under township organization, if any townships do not coincide with the bounds of organized towns, such townships also hold their election for school trustee on the second Saturday in April. And if a township lies partly in two or more counties, it nevertheless elects school trustees, and is governed in school matters as if it lay wholly in one county and was not coincident in its bounds with an organized town.

In counties not under township organization, the county board divides the county into election precincts. Each precinct elects as many justices and constables as a town of equal population.

Q. How many kinds of townships are there in Illinois?

III. THE COUNTY.

Q. What political division of the State is larger than the town?

A. The county.

Q. In what county do you live? How large is it? Is it under township organization? If so, give the names of its towns. Give its bounds. Name its seat. What is a county seat?

A. It is the city or village where the court-house and county offices are, and where the county business is done.

COUNTY OFFICERS—THEIR TERMS OF OFFICE.

Q. Name the officers of a county and give the term of each.

A. County clerk, clerk of the circuit court, recorder, county judge, probate judge, State's attorney, sheriff, superintendent of schools, treasurer, surveyor, and coroner; term, four years. In counties under township organization, supervisors; one or more from each town, and one or more from each city in the county (the number from cities being determined in the same way as in towns); term, one year.

In counties not under township organization, instead of supervisors there are three commissioners, elected by the whole county for a term of three years.

THE COUNTY BOARD—POWERS AND DUTIES.

Q. What officers constitute the county board?

A. The supervisors or commissioners.

Q. How many meetings do the supervisors hold in a year?

A. Two regular meetings, namely, on the second Monday in July and the second Tuesday in September; and special meetings whenever one-third of their number ask for such meetings.

Q. How does the county board organize for business?

A. The first meeting of the year is called to order by the county clerk, when the supervisors proceed to elect one of their number chairman for the succeeding year.

Q. What are the duties of the chairman?

A. To appoint the committees and preside over the meetings of the board.

Q. What can you say about the committees?

A. A committee consists of three or more members of the board, whose special duty it is to look after some branch of the county business. Thus, the members of the committee for the poor see that the county farm for the support of the county's paupers is properly managed, and that the paupers are properly fed, clothed and housed. They also examine and allow or disallow bills for the support of the poor. This is called "auditing bills." Nearly all the county business is divided among the committees of the board, but each committee must report all its proposed acts to the board for its approval before the acts can be done.

Q. What are some of the duties of the whole board?

A. To erect and furnish a court-house, jail, and other necessary county buildings. To levy special taxes for this and other purposes.

To fix the pay of county officers, which can not be changed during the term for which the officers are elected.

To take measures for prosecuting and defending the lawsuits of the county.

To select grand jurors, and prepare a list from which the circuit clerk may draw petit jurors.

To examine all bills against the county, and see that none are paid except those that are just.

To examine the accounts of the county treasurer and count the money in the treasury twice a year.

To publish in a paper of the county after each meeting a full report of all their acts.

The supervisors must hold their meetings with open doors, and, if possible, in the court-house.

They can not levy a tax of more than 75 cents on $100 valuation for ordinary county expenses, nor more than 100 cents on $100 valuation to pay a county debt, existing at the time of the adoption of the present State constitution, nor contract a bonded debt for the county, without first submitting the question of such tax or debt to a vote of the people.

Q. Why is the county board required to hold its meetings with open doors, and to publish accounts of its proceedings?

THE GRAND JURY.

Q. What can you say about a grand jury?

A. A grand jury consists of twenty-three men. It is their duty to examine evidence against those accused of crime, and if the evidence is strong enough, to advise the court to put the accused on trial. The grand jury's advice in such a case consists in giving the court a paper called an "indictment," in which the criminal is named and his crime is described. A majority of the grand jury must vote in favor of an indictment before it can be presented to the court. The grand jury hears no evidence in defense, and its meetings are not open to the public.

PETIT JURY.

Q. What can you say of a petit jury?

A. A petit jury consists of twelve men. It is their duty to hear the evidence on both sides of every case brought before them, and to decide the case according to the weight of the evidence and the law that applies to that particular case. The law is explained to them by the judge. Their decision is called a "verdict." A verdict can not be given unless all the jury vote for it.

COUNTY AND PROBATE COURT.

Q. Are the offices of county judge and probate judge filled by one man or two men in your county?

Q. In what case are these offices separate?

A. In counties of 50,000 inhabitants two men may be elected to fill these offices. In counties of less than 50,000 inhabitants, one man is elected to perform the duties of both offices. In this case he is called simply the "county judge," and his court is called the "county court."

Q. What jurisdiction have probate courts?

A. They have original jurisdiction in matters relating to wills, the settlement of estates of deceased persons, apprentices, guardians of minors, and conservators of the insane and the imbecile.

Q. What is meant by "original jurisdiction?" By "exclusive jurisdiction?"

A. When a court has original jurisdiction in any matters, suits about those matters may be commenced in that court.

When a court has exclusive jurisdiction in any mat-

2

ters, suits about such matters must be commenced in that court alone.

Q. What jurisdiction have county courts?

A. They have exclusive jurisdiction in suits for the collection of taxes by sale of real estate, and concurrent jurisdiction with circuit courts in civil matters, in all cases like those brought before justices of the peace, if the amount in dispute does not exceed $1,000, and in criminal matters, if the punishment may not be imprisonment in the penitentiary or death. County courts have also concurrent jurisdiction with circuit courts in cases appealed from justices of the peace and police magistrates.

Q. What is meant by "concurrent jurisdiction?"

A. Matters in which two or more courts have concurrent jurisdiction can be brought before either of such courts. If A gives me a note for any sum less than $200, and when it is due refuses to pay, I can sue him before a justice of the peace, or in the county, or the circuit court, for all these have concurrent jurisdiction in such a case.

Q. What are civil and criminal matters?

(See the chapter on The Town.)

Q. What is it "to appeal" a case?

A. It is to carry it, after trial, to a higher court for a new trial. The higher court, in such an event, is said to have "appellate jurisdiction."

COUNTY AND PROBATE JUDGES.

Q. What are the duties of county and probate judges?

A. To preside over the county and probate courts in their respective counties.

COUNTY CLERK.

Q. Who is county clerk in your county?

Q. What are some of the duties of the county clerk?

A. To attend the sessions of the county court, and make a record, in books kept for the purpose, of whatever is done by the court.

To keep a record of all the acts of the county board.

To keep a record of all the orders for money drawn on the county treasurer.

After every general election, to count, with the aid of two justices of the peace, the votes as returned to him by the judges of election in the various towns and precincts of the county, and to send the result to the Secretary of State.

To issue marriage licenses.

To compute the tax of every person in the county, enter it in proper books, and issue these books to the collectors.

Q. What books must the clerk have before he can compute the tax?

A. He must have the assessor's books, for in these the value of each person's property is set down.

Q. How is the rate per cent. of taxation determined? (See your Arithmetic.)

Q. What is a general election?

A. An election where any State officer is chosen.

SHERIFF.

Q. Name the sheriff in your county?

Q. For how long a term is a sheriff elected?

Q. What are some of a sheriff's duties?

A. To attend all the sessions of the county and circuit courts, to preserve order in the same, and to execute the commands of the court.

To serve writs, summonses, subpœnas and other judi-cial papers.

To prevent disorderly conduct wherever he is, and to arrest offenders against the law.

To have charge of the court-house and jail, to take criminals condemned to imprisonment to the penitentiary or house of correction, and to hang criminals condemned to death.

STATE'S ATTORNEY.

Q. Name the State's attorney in your county?

Q. What are some of his duties?

A. To prosecute criminals. To draw indictments for the grand jury.

To act as attorney for his county in all suits brought for or against it.

To act as counsel for all county officers and justices of the peace in matters relating to their duties as representatives of the people.

Q. Who is a criminal?

A. One who has offended against a public law.

Q. What is it "to prosecute" a criminal?

A. To prosecute a criminal is to have him arrested an l brought into court, to bring evidence before the court intended to prove him guilty, and to ask the court to have him punished, if guilty. All criminals have a right to be tried by a jury.

CORONER.

Q. What are the duties of a coroner?

A. To examine, with the aid of a jury, the body of any person killed by accident or having died from any mysterious cause, and to report such examination to the county clerk.

To arrest, if necessary to prevent escape, any one suspected of killing the deceased.

To act as sheriff, if the sheriff's office becomes vacant, or if the sheriff is interested in any suit.

CIRCUIT CLERK AND RECORDER OF DEEDS.

Q. What other offices, besides those of county and probate judge, are sometimes united and filled by one man?

A. The offices of clerk of the circuit court and recorder of deeds.

Q. Where are these offices united and where separate?

A. In counties of less than 60,000 inhabitants they are united. In counties of 60,000, or more, they are separate.

Q. What are some of the duties of clerk of the circuit court?

A. To attend the sessions of the circuit court in his county, and make a record in books provided for the purpose of all the proceedings of that court.

To keep an account of the costs of suits, such as fees of the sheriff, clerk, and witnesses.

To issue process, that is, to write down the orders of the court, and give these orders to the sheriff and his assistants to execute.

Q. Who pay the costs of suits?

A. Generally the persons against whom suits are decided.

Q. What are the principal duties of recorders?

A. To obtain suitable books, and, when requested, to record in these, deeds, mortgages, and all other papers relating to the title to land, and to record also chattel mortgages.

DEEDS.

Q. What is a deed?

A. It is a writing showing that a certain piece of land described in it is the property of the person named in the writing as owner or grantee.

RECORDING DEEDS.

Q. What is "recording" a deed?

A. It is making a copy of it in one of the recorder's books.

Q. What are deeds recorded for?

A. That the recorder's books may show who owns the land, if the deeds are lost.

MORTGAGES.

Q. What is a mortgage?

A. It is a writing showing that a certain piece of land, or other property, will become the property of a person named in the writing and called the mortgagee, if the owner, or mortgagor, of the land or other property, does not pay the mortgagee a certain sum of money at a given time. A chattel mortgage is a mortgage of other property than land.

TREASURER.

Q. For what term is the county treasurer elected? (See page 22.)

Q. Who is treasurer in your county?

Q. What are some of a treasurer's duties?

A. To receive and take care of all money paid for taxes, and to pay it out on the order of the county board, or in the manner specially provided by law.

To keep books of his accounts as treasurer, and have them always open to the inspection of the public.

To report to the county board at each of its regular sessions all sums of money received and paid out by him.

SUPERINTENDENT OF SCHOOLS.

Q. Name the superintendent of schools in your county. When was he elected? When does his term expire?

Q. What are some of his duties?

A. To visit schools if so directed by the county board, notice the manner of teaching, branches taught, text books used, and the general condition of schools. To instruct teachers in the best methods of teaching. To hold county teachers' institutes. To hold examination for teachers' license at least once every three months. To decide disputes on questions of school law. To divide the money received from the State among the townships in proportion to the children under twenty-one years of age in each township. To examine and approve the bonds and books and accounts of township school treasurers before issuing money to them. To remove from office directors who do not perform their duties properly, and to order new elections to fill such vacancies. To visit each school in the county, at least once a year. To report to the State superintendent whatever facts the latter needs for his report to the governor.

THE DEPARTMENTS OF COUNTY GOVERNMENT.

Q. What departments has county government?

A. The same as town government ; namely, legislative, executive and judicial.

Q. Explain each?

A. The county board is the legislative or law-making department. It adopts measures for the benefit of the whole county, such as those for the erection of county buildings, for the care of the county's paupers, and so forth.

The county clerk, treasurer, recorder, superintendent of schools, form the executive department. They execute the laws made by the county board (and State legislature). The committees of the county board, acting as committees, also perform executive duties ; that is, they carry into effect the measures or laws passed by the whole board.

The judicial department consists of the county judge, sheriff, State's attorney, coroner, and county clerk when he acts as clerk of the county court. It is the duty of these officers to enforce obedience to the laws made by the county board and the State legislature. The circuit clerk is not, strictly speaking, a member of either department of the county government, although he is elected by the county. He is an officer of the circuit court, which will be described hereafter.

Q. State the relation of the three departments ?

A. The legislative department, by a vote of a majority of its members, commands that certain things be done. The executive officers do the things commanded, or cause them to be done.

If these officers are resisted or hindered in their duties, the judicial officers help them by punishing the persons resisting or hindering.

COUNTIES NOT UNDER TOWNSHIP ORGANIZATION.

Q. What can you say of county government in counties not under township organization ?

A. The county board consists of three commissioners, elected for a term of three years. They have nearly all the powers of county supervisors, and have, besides, the powers of all town officers, except school officers. They hold five regular meetings a year. The other officers of such counties are the same as in counties

under township organization, and they have the same
duties to perform, except that the sheriff acts also as
county collector.

COOK COUNTY.

The county board of Cook County is composed of fifteen members elected annually, ten of whom are elected
from Chicago, and five from the towns outside of Chicago. Voters may vote for one of the candidates to be
president of the board.

COMPENSATION—BONDS—OATH.

Q. How is the pay of officers in all kinds of counties
determined ?

A. The county boards fix the amount of compensation of each officer.

Q. What must officers do before entering on the duties
of their offices ?

A. Such officers as have public money committed to
their care must give bonds for their good behavior and
faithfulness in office, and all must take an oath that they
will support the constitution of the United States and
the constitution of Illinois, and will faithfully perform
the duties of their offices.

IV. THE STATE.

THE LEGISLATURE.

Q. In treating of the government of the town and of
the county, which department was described first ?

A. The legislative or law-making.

Q. Pursuing the same plan with the State, what is our
next topic ?

A. The legislature of Illinois. (The legislature is also
called the " general assembly.")

Q. Describe it, and explain the election of its members ?

A. The legislature consists of two parts, known as
the " lower house " and " upper house." Members of the

C

lower house are called representatives. Members of the upper house are called senators.

ELECTION OF MEMBERS OF THE LEGISLATURE.

The State is divided into fifty-one parts called "senatorial districts." Each of these districts elects one senator for a term of four years, and three representatives for a term of two years.

Q. What is "minority representation?"

A. In voting for representatives, every voter may cast three votes for one candidate, or one and a half for each of two, or one vote for each of three candidates. It is called "minority representation" because the party having a minority in a district, by casting all their votes for one candidate may sometimes elect him.

Q. How large a part (at least) of the whole number of voters must the minority be in order to elect one candidate?

MEETING OF THE LEGISLATURE.

Q. How often does the legislature meet?

A. Once in two years, unless called by the governor to meet oftener in extra session.

Q. When does its regular session begin?

A. On Wednesday after the first Monday in January following the election of representatives.

Q. Where does it meet?

A. In the capitol building, in Springfield.

DUTIES OF LIEUTENANT-GOVERNOR AND SPEAKER.

Q. What officers preside over the two houses?

A. The lieutenant-governor presides over the senate, an officer called the "speaker," elected from their own number by the representatives at the beginning of the session, presides over the house of representatives.

Q. What other important duty is performed by the speaker of the house?

A. He appoints the committees of the house.

Q. What can you say about committees of the legislature?

A. A committee consists of three or more members, whose duty it is to attend to some particular subject of legislation. For example, the committee on education has charge of all matters relating to the public schools of the State, and it is the duty of this committee to advise the legislature what to do for the schools. The committee's advice to the legislature is called its "report."

Q. What is the chief rule for selecting members of committees?

A. A majority of each committee is taken from the political party which has a majority in the house to which the committee belongs.

Q. Why is the appointment of committees a very important duty?

A. Because nearly all the work of a legislature is done by its committees. Reports of committees are nearly always adopted by the legislature without material change.

DUTIES OF THE LEGISLATURE.

Q. What are the duties of the whole legislature?

A. To levy such taxes, make such appropriations, and enact such laws as are necessary for the welfare of the State. To impeach State officers; that is, to arraign and try them and deprive them of office for misconduct in office.

Q. What is an appropriation?

A. A sum of money directed by the legislature to be used for a certain purpose; as, for the support of the asylum for the insane, or the penitentiary, or the State normal schools.

Q. What counties compose the senatorial district in which you live? (See page 60.)

Who is senator from your district? Who are representatives?

THE EXECUTIVE DEPARTMENT.

Q. What officers constitute the executive department of Illinois?

A. Governor, lieutenant-governor, secretary of State, auditor, treasurer, superintendent of public instruction, and attorney-general.

Q. For what terms are they elected?

A. The treasurer for two years, the others for four years.

The constitution declares that the treasurer shall not serve two consecutive terms. Why?

Q. Before entering on their duties what must they do?

A. Take the oath of office by swearing to support the constitutions of Illinois and the United States, and to perform faithfully the duties of their offices. All other State officers take the same oath.

THE GOVERNOR.

Q. What are the duties and powers of the governor?

A. To see that the laws made by the legislature are executed.

To send to the legislature, when it meets, a message, giving an account of the condition of the State and its wants; recommending the levying of sufficient tax to defray the expenses of the State government; and specifying what new laws he thinks ought to be enacted, and what old laws repealed. To approve bills passed by the legislature if he wishes them to become laws.

The governor has power to reprieve criminals condemned to death, and to pardon those imprisoned in the penitentiary.

He is commander-in-chief of the State militia when it is not in the service of the United States.

He appoints, with the consent of the senate, certain State officers.

He may veto a bill passed by the legislature.

Q. Can a bill become a law if it is vetoed by the governor?

A. Yes, if it is afterwards passed by a majority of two-thirds of both houses.

Q. Can a bill become a law in any other way without the governor's approval?

A. Yes. If the governor does not return a bill to the house in which it originated within ten days from the time when he received it; or, if the legislature prevents his returning the bill by adjourning, and if he does not thereupon file the bill with his objections in the office of the secretary of State within ten days after adjournment, the bill will become a law.

Q. What compensation does the governor receive?

A. $6,000 per year, with the use of the executive mansion.

WHO SUCCEEDS IF THE GOVERNOR'S OFFICE BECOMES VACANT.

Q. Who succeeds to the office of governor if it becomes vacant before the end of a term?

A. The lieutenant-governor.

Q. What is the lieutenant-governor's salary?

A. $1,000 per year.

Q. Who would succeed the lieutenant-governor if he should vacate the governor's office ?

A. The president *pro tem.* of the senate. (The president *pro tem.* is a member of the senate elected to preside in the absence of the lieutenant-governor.)

Q. Who would succeed the president of the senate ?

A. The speaker of the house.

SECRETARY OF STATE.

Q. What are the principal duties of the secretary of State ?

A. To call the house of representatives to order, and preside till a temporary chairman is elected. (The latter presides while the house votes for speaker.)

To safely keep all public acts, laws, and resolutions of the legislature.

To care for public property in the capital.

To certify to the correctness of laws when they are published.

To take care of the seal of State.

To issue registration blanks to judges of election previous to every general election.

To issue charters to corporations.

To have charge of the public standards of weights and measures.

To report biennially to the governor the business of his office.

Q. What security must the secretary give for the faithful performance of his duties ?

A. He must give a bond for $100,000.

Q. What is his salary ?

A. $3,500 per year.

AUDITOR.

Q. What are the chief duties of auditor?

A. To examine all bills presented for payment out of the State treasury, and to approve such as are legal.

To keep an account of all bills due the State, and all sums of money paid into the State treasury.

To ascertain the condition of all insurance companies doing business in the State; learning whether they have means sufficient to keep the promises that they have made to those whose lives or property they have insured; and if any have not, to revoke their certificates, or to inform the attorney-general, who will then ask a court to have such companies stopped from doing any further business in the State.

To aid the governor and treasurer in computing the rate per cent. of taxation necessary to raise the annual revenue fixed by the legislature.

To report biennially to the governor the transactions of his office.

Q. What security must the auditor give?

A. A bond for $50,000.

Q. What is his salary?

A. $3,500 a year.

TREASURER.

Q. What are the principal duties of the treasurer?

A. To receive and safely keep all money belonging to the State.

To pay out no money except on the order of the auditor.

To report monthly to the auditor all sums of money received and paid out.

To report biennially to the governor all his official acts.

Q. What security must the treasurer give for the faithful performance of his duty?

A. A bond for $500,000, and more, if the governor so requires. His salary is $3,500 per year.

SUPERINTENDENT OF PUBLIC INSTRUCTION.

Q. What are some of the duties of the superintendent of public instruction?

A. To consult with leading teachers on methods of instruction. To advise and instruct county superintendents in respect to their duties. To give opinions on school laws when properly requested. To pay promptly to the proper officers all money coming into his hands as superintendent. To stop the payment of money to officers or teachers who refuse to conform to the requirements of law. To report biennially to the governor, stating what has been done for the benefit of the schools of the State, in what ways their condition may be improved, and what changes should be made in the school laws. The superintendent must give a bond for $25,000. His salary is $3,500 per year.

ATTORNEY-GENERAL.

Q. What are some of the duties of the attorney-general?

A. To act as attorney for the people or the State in suits before the supreme court. To act as attorney for the State officers in suits relating to their official duties. To advise State officers on questions of State constitutional law, when such law relates to their duties. To advise the legislature concerning constitutional questions when requested. To see that sums of money intended for State institutions are used as intended. The attorney-general's bond is for $10,000. His salary is $3,500 a year.

RETURNING BOARD.

Q. Who constitute the State returning board?

A. The secretary of State, auditor, treasurer, and attorney-general.

Q. What is the duty of the returning board?

A. After every general election, to count the votes returned to them by the county clerks.

STATE BOARD OF EQUALIZATION.

The State board of equalization consists of one member from each congressional district in the State. The term is four years. The board meets on the second Tuesday in August, annually, at Springfield, to equalize assessments in the various counties of the State. Its members receive $5.00 per day for time actually spent about their duties, and 10 cents per mile of necessary travel in going to and returning from the capital.

STATE BOARD OF AGRICULTURE.

The State board of agriculture consists of a president, and one vice-president from each congressional district in the State, and of the last ex-president of the board. The board is elected biennially, on Wednesday of the State fair week, on the State fair grounds, by a convention consisting of two or three delegates from each county in the State, who have power to cast three votes for their county. These delegates are chosen by the agricultural societies in the respective counties, or, in counties where no such societies exist, by the county board. The State board of agriculture has control of the department of agriculture, and of the State fairs and stock shows.

APPOINTED OFFICERS.

OFFICERS APPOINTED BY GOVERNOR WITH CONSENT OF SENATE.

Q. What State officers are appointed by the governor with the consent of the senate?

A. Three canal commissioners, five commissioners of public charities, three penitentiary commissioners for each penitentiary, nineteen justices of the peace for the city of Chicago, the seven members composing the State board of health, chief grain inspectors, notaries public, three railway and warehouse commissioners, three trustees for each of the State charitable institutions, and three for the State reform school, one person at the stock yards near Chicago, one at Peoria, and one at those in East St. Louis, to prevent cruelty to animals, and one public administrator in each county.

COMMISSION OF CLAIMS.

The commission of claims consists of three persons learned in law, selected from at least two political parties, appointed by the Governor with the consent of the senate, and holding office four years. The commission meets at the Capitol on the first Monday in August each year. It sits as a court to try claims against the State and the State institutions, and certain other claims. Its members receive $15.00 per day for a session of not exceeding ninety days in each year.

OFFICERS APPOINTED BY GOVERNOR ALONE.

Q. What other officers are appointed by the governor?

A. Commissioner of deeds, printer expert, adjutant general, and all commissioned officers of the State militia.

DUTIES OF OFFICERS APPOINTED BY GOVERNOR WITH CONSENT OF SENATE.

Q. State the duties, terms of office, and pay of each of the above officers.

A. The *canal commissioners* have charge of the Illinois and Michigan canal, and of the locks, dams and improvements in navigation of the Illinois and Little Wabash rivers. Their term is two years. Their pay is $5 per day for the time actually employed. They must each, except the treasurer of the board, give bonds for $25,000. The commissioner who acts as treasurer must give bonds for $50,000.

It is the duty of *commissioners of public charities* to visit, at least twice a year, the State asylums for the deaf and dumb, the blind, the insane, and the school for feeble-minded children, the soldiers' orphans' home, and the State reform school, and to see that these institutions are properly conducted. Their term is five years. They receive no pay, but their expenses are repaid to them by the State.

The *Chicago justices of the peace* perform the same duties as other justices, and derive their pay from fees regulated by law. They hold office for a term of four years.

The *penitentiary commissioners* have power to appoint a warden for the penitentiary at a salary of $2,500, a deputy warden at $1,800, a chaplain at $1,500, a physician at $1,500 per year, and, with the advice of the warden, such other officers as may be necessary, at salaries fixed by the commissioners.

It is the duty of the commissioners to care for the penitentiary, and to this end to meet at the penitentiary once every month, and to receive reports from the warden and other officers. They are required to report biennially to the governor.

Their term is six years. They must give bonds for $25,000. Their salary is $1,500 per year.

One of the most important duties of the *State board of health* is to prevent the introduction of contagious diseases into the State. The members receive no pay, except for expenses. They may appoint a secretary at a salary fixed by themselves, but his salary and their expenses together must not exceed $5,000 per year. Their term is seven years.

It is the duty of the *railway and warehouse commissioners* to examine the condition and management of all railways and warehouses in the State, and all matters relating to railways and warehouses as far as they affect the welfare of the people ; and to report annually to the governor, informing him whether warehouses and railways are observing the laws of the State made for their regulation. The commissioners must give bonds for $20,000. Their salary is $3,500. Their term is two years. They can appoint a secretary at a salary of $1,500 per year.

Chief grain inspectors have charge of the inspection of grain in warehouses, obey the instructions of the railway commissioners, and receive salaries fixed by them. Their term is two years.

In all cities where there is State inspection of grain, the railway and warehouse commissioners appoint a *State weigh-master* and such assistants as may be necessary, whose duty it is to inspect scales, and supervise the weighing of grain or other property.

The trustees of the State charitable and correctional institutions have power, and it is their duty, to appoint a superintendent for each institution, and to make rules for the government of the same. They receive no pay except for their expenses. Their term is six years.

The duty of the *officers appointed to prevent cruelty to animals* has been stated above. They hold office two years, and receive $1,200 a year.

One *public administrator* is appointed in each county, whose duty it is to settle the estate of any person who dies in the county and leaves property, but no heirs or creditors.

Notaries public have authority to administer oaths, take acknowledgment of legal instruments, such as deeds and mortgages, and to do some other acts, such as writing down the evidence of witnesses, called " taking depositions." These depositions have the same effect when read in court as evidence taken in court.

DUTIES OF OFFICERS APPOINTED BY GOVERNOR ALONE.

Commissioners of deeds are officers appointed by the governor of this State, but residing in other States. They have authority to do about the same acts as are done by notaries public, which acts are of binding force in Illinois, though done in other States. All the above officers are paid in fees fixed by law.

The *printer expert* is a man of at least six years' experience as a practical printer, whose duty it is to examine the State contracts for printing, to see that the State is not cheated. His pay is $6 per day for the time actually spent about his duties.

The *adjutant-general* is the officer through whom the governor, as commander-in-chief of the State militia, issues his orders to the militia. The adjutant-general receives $1,500 per year.

Q. What is the acknowledgment of a deed ?

A. It is the act of the person who signed the deed, in

going before a notary public or other officer and declaring that he signed the deed.

STATE MILITIA.

Q. What is the State militia?

A. All able-bodied men between eighteen and forty-five years of age are liable to be called upon to serve as soldiers. These constitute the State militia. This term is usually applied only to those who voluntarily form themselves into companies and regiments and receive arms from the State.

JUDICIAL DEPARTMENT.
CIRCUIT COURTS.

Q. What is the judicial department of a State?

A. The judicial department of a State consists of those officers whose duty it is to explain and apply the laws of the State.

Q. Have we learned that the subdivisions of the State have judicial departments?

A. Yes. Towns and precincts have justices of the peace and constables. Counties have county judges, clerks, sheriffs, and State's attorneys.

Q. What court is next above the county court?

A. The circuit court.

Q. What can you say about the circuit courts of Illinois?

A. The counties of the State, Cook county being excepted, are arranged by the legislature in thirteen divisions, called circuits. Cook county alone constitutes a circuit.

CIRCUIT COURT OFFICERS.

In each circuit, except Cook County, three judges are elected once in six years. Two of these act as circuit judges. The third acts as one of the judges of the appellate courts. Court is held at least one term in a year in each county of the circuit. The number of judges in Cook County, at any given time, depends on the population of the county, and is fixed by act of the legislature.

Q. Who are the other officers of the circuit courts?

A. The sheriffs and circuit clerks and their assistants, and masters-in-chancery in their respective counties.

Q. Who else assist the judge in the performance of his duties?

A. The petit and grand juries.

Q. What jurisdiction have circuit courts?

A. They have original jurisdiction in all criminal offences against the laws of Illinois, and in all civil disputes between citizens of the State. They have appellate jurisdiction in cases tried before justices of the peace and the county court.

Q. What are criminal offenses and civil disputes? (See page 18.)

APPELLATE COURTS.

Q. What are the courts next above the circuit courts?

A. The appellate courts.

Q. Describe these?

A. The State is divided into four apppellate court districts. Each district has three judges. These are appointed by the supreme court from the judges elected in the circuits. Each district has a clerk, elected for a term of six years. The sheriff of the county in which the court is held must attend the sessions of the court or appoint a deputy to do so.

Q. What kinds of cases can be taken to the appellate courts?

A. Nearly all kinds of cases, except criminal cases

called "felonies," may be taken by appeal to the appellate courts. Cases of felony and a few other cases must be appealed directly to the supreme court.

Q. What about the decisions of appellate courts?

A. In all cases where less than $1,000 is in dispute their decisions are final. If the sum in dispute is $1,000 or more, an appeal may be taken from the appellate to the supreme court.

THE SUPREME COURT.

Q. What can you say of the supreme court?

A. The State is divided into three grand divisions for the purpose of holding terms of the supreme court. The court consists of seven judges, elected for a term of nine years. The State is divided into seven districts for the election of these judges, each district electing one. Each of the three grand divisions elects a clerk for a term of six years.

Q. What jurisdiction has the supreme court?

A. It has original jurisdiction in cases relating to the revenues of the State and in respect to two or three other matters, and appellate jurisdiction in civil cases involving $1,000 or more, and in criminal cases amounting to felony. Its decisions are final, except in cases of conflict between Illinois law and United States law. In such cases appeal can be taken to the supreme court of the United States.

PAY OF OFFICERS OF THE JUDICIAL DEPARTMENT.

Q. What are the salaries of the officers of the above courts?

A. Circuit judges receive $3,500 per year, except in Cook county, where they receive $7,000. Circuit clerks receive salaries fixed by the county boards. Appellate judges receive the same pay as circuit judges. Judges of the supreme court receive $5,000 per year. Appellate and supreme court clerks and masters-in-chancery receive their pay in fees regulated by law.

All these officers must take the usual official oath, and the clerks must give bonds.

V. CITIES.

THEIR GOVERNMENT.

Q. What other political units are there in Illinois besides towns, townships, and counties?

A. Cities and villages.

Q. How many kinds of cities are there?

A. Two.

Q. State the difference between them?

A. One is organized and governed according to a general law made by the legislature for the benefit of such cities as may vote to organize under it.

The other is organized and governed in accordance with a special charter granted to it by the legislature.

Q. What is a charter?

A. It is a grant of certain privileges, and is, besides, intended for the government of the corporation to which these privileges are given.

OFFICERS AND THEIR DUTIES.

Q. Describe the government of the first kind of cities?

A. Its legislative department consists of a body called the common council. The city is divided into a certain number of parts called "wards." Each of these elects two members of the council for a term of two years.

The chief executive officer is a *mayor*, elected for a term of two years.

Other officers elected by the people are clerk, attorney, treasurer, police magistrate, and sometimes city judge.

Besides these, the council may provide for the election by the people, or the appointment by the mayor, with the consent of the council, of a collector, marshal, or superintendent of police, superintendent of streets, corporation counsel, and such other officers as the council may deem necessary.

Q. What are the council's duties?

A. To enact such ordinances and levy such taxes as are necessary for the city's welfare.

To approve or reject the mayor's appointments of city officers.

To take some action on the mayor's suggestions.

To receive petitions of citizens.

Q. What is an ordinance?

A. A law passed by a city council.

Q. What are the mayor's duties?

A. To preside at the meetings of the council.

To see that the measures passed by the council are executed.

To appoint, with the council's consent, certain officers.

He may veto measures passed by the council, but if the council afterward pass the same by a two-thirds majority, they become laws.

Q. State the principal duties of the other city officers.

A. The *clerk* keeps a record of the acts of the council.

The *marshal* has command of the policemen, and with them preserves public order, by arresting and putting in jail all disorderly persons.

The *superintendent of streets* keeps the streets and sidewalks in repair.

The *comptroller* prevents the city from being robbed

by its officers, by examining the accounts of all officers who collect, pay out, or receive any of the city's money.

The *corporation counsel* is the chief officer of the law department of the city.

The *police magistrate's* duties are the same as those of a justice of the peace (See page 18.)

The *attorney, treasurer* and *collector* perform about the same duties for the city as the corresponding officers do for the county.

Q. What can you say about the pay of city officers?

A. It is fixed by the council.

Q. What can you say of the government of cities under special charters?

A. As each has its own charter, no two such cities are governed exactly alike, but all are more or less similar in their government to cities organized under the general law.

VI. VILLAGES.

Q. What can you say of the government of villages?

A. Under a general law of the State, villages as well as cities may organize and have a government separate from that of the township in which they are located.

Such village government consists of a president of the village, elected annually, a board of six trustees, three of whom are elected annually, and such officers as the trustees may appoint.

The president and board have about the same powers and duties as mayor and council have in cities.

VII. GOVERNMENT OF THE UNITED STATES.

CONGRESS.

Q. What is the legislature or law-making body of the United States called ?

A. It is called Congress.

Q. Tell about its meetings ?

A. It holds one regular session a year, and extra sessions when called by the president. It meets in regular session, in Washington, on the first Monday in December.

Q. Describe Congress, and tell how its members are chosen ?

A. It consists of two houses, the senate and the house of representatives.

Each State is entitled to two senators. Senators are elected by the State legislatures for a term of six years.

The number of representatives that a State is entitled to depends on its population.

Once in ten years, that is, after each census, congress fixes the total number of members that the house of representatives shall have during the next ten years. Let the whole population of the United States be a dividend, and the number of representatives a divisor ; the quotient will be the number of persons entitled to one representative.

Divide the population of a State by this quotient and the number of representatives the State is entitled to will be obtained.

The legislature divides the State into districts equal in number to the representatives the State is entitled to. One representative is elected from each district every two years.

Q. Who presides over the senate?

A. The vice-president.

Q. How does the house ot representatives organize for business?

A. By the election of a speaker, whose business it is to preside and appoint the house committees.

Q. What are the powers and duties of congress?

(See U. S. Constitution, Article I., Section 8.)

Q. What is the salary of senators and representatives?

A. $5,000 per year.

Q. Who are the present senators from Illinois?

In what congressional district do you live? (See page 58.)

What counties comprise your district?

Who is its present representative in congress?

When was he elected?

Who were the opposing candidates?

Who is the present speaker of the house ot representatives?

How many congressional districts are there in Illinois? (See page 59.)

Of how many members does the house of representatives now consist?

A. 325.

Q. Do territories have any representatives in congress?

A. Each territory is entitled to one delegate in the

house, who has the right to speak on questions relating to his territory, but can not vote on any question.

EXECUTIVE DEPARTMENT.

Q. Who constitute the executive department of the government of the United States?

A. The president, vice-president and cabinet officers.

Q. How are the first two elected?

(See Article II., Section 1, and the 12th Amendment to the U. S. Constitution.)

Q. What are their salaries?

A. President, $50,000; vice-president, $8,000 per year.

Q. Name the cabinet officers?

A. Secretary of State, secretary of the treasury, secretary of war, secretary of the navy, secretary of the interior, postmaster-general, and attorney-general.

Q. What general duties do cabinet officers perform?

A. They advise the president, and assist him in executing the laws made by congress.

Q. What are the president's duties?

(See U. S. Constitution, Article II., Sections 2 and 3.)

Q. What are the special duties of the secretary of State?

A. To look after the relations of the United States with foreign countries, and to have charge of the public archives.

Q. What are the principal duties of the secretary of the interior?

A. To attend to the relations of Indian tribes to the government, to superintend public lands, to issue patents.

Q. What are the special duties of the other cabinet officers? (Their names indicate their duties.)

Q. What is the salary of a cabinet officer?

A. $8,000 per year.

Q. Name the present president, vice-president, and cabinet officers?

When were the first two elected?

Who were the opposing candidates?

Q. Whom do we mean when we speak of the "administration?"

A. The president and his cabinet.

Q. Is it necessary to have the names of candidates for president and vice-president printed on a presidential ticket?

(See 12th Amendment of U. S. Constitution.)

Could the electors be chosen in any other way than by a direct vote of the people?

Who succeeds to the presidency if it becomes vacant?

(See Article II., Section 1 of U. S. Constitution.)

The president *pro tem.* of the senate would succeed the vice-president, and the speaker of the house would succeed the president of the senate in the presidential office.

JUDICIAL DEPARTMENT.

Q. Describe the judicial department of the United States?

A. It consists of one supreme court, nine circuit courts, and sixty-five district courts. The supreme court has one chief justice and eight associate justices. The circuit courts have each one judge. There are fifty-three district judges. The district courts have, besides judges, district attorneys, marshals (who have substantially the same duties as sheriffs), clerks, and assistants of each. All the judges are appointed by the president, with the consent of the senate, and hold office during life or good behavior.

Q. What salaries do United States judges receive?

A. The chief justice receives a salary of $10,500, the associates, $10,000 ; the circuit judges, $6,000 ; and the district judges $3,500 to $4,500.

Q. What jurisdiction has the supreme court?

(See Constitution, Article III., Section 2, Paragraph 2.)

Q. What are the principal duties of circuit and district courts?

A. To try offenders against the laws made by congress, and to hear suits between citizens of different States.

Q. Who is the present chief justice?

Who is the circuit judge in your circuit?

Who is the district judge in your district?

THE ARMY AND NAVY.

Q. What can you say of the officers of the army and navy?

A. They are nearly all educated for their duties at the expense of the government in the military and naval academies at West Point and Annapolis. They are commissioned, that is, appointed to their places, by the president.

THE CIVIL SERVICE.

Q. What is the civil service of the United States?

A. The "civil service," comprises all officers of the national government, who are appointed by the president or his subordinates, except the officers of the army and the navy.

Q. Name some of the officers of the civil service, and give their duties?

A. *Ministers.* It is the duty of a minister to reside

at the capital of the country to which he is sent, to protect citizens of his own country when abroad, and to see if possible that the country in which he resides as minister, and his own, maintain friendship for each other.

Consuls. Their principal duties are to look after the foreign trade of their own country, and to settle disputes between the citizens of their own country, when the latter are abroad.

Internal revenue officers. It is their chief duty to collect the tax on liquors and tobacco.

Custom-house officers. They collect the tax laid on foreign goods brought into the United States.

Postmasters, mail carriers and *lighthouse-keepers* are also members of the civil service.

Q. Who is the present American minister to England?

Who is the English minister in Washington?

Who is collector of customs at the port of Chicago?

Who is the internal revenue collector in your district?

Who is postmaster at your post office?

Do you know any other members of the civil service?

Q. Do you know the meaning of the expression, "Civil Service Reform?"

VIII.   MISCELLANEOUS.

NATIONAL POLITICAL CONVENTION.

Q. Tell how candidates are put in nomination by a political party for the offices of president and vice-president?

A. The national committee, consisting of at least one

member from each State in the Union, publishes a call, announcing that on a certain day and in a certain city, there will be held a national convention of delegates from all the States (and sometimes the territories) to nominate candidates and adopt a platform.

Each State committee then publishes a call for a State convention to appoint as many delegates to the national convention as the State may be entitled to.

The county committees in each State then issue calls for county conventions to appoint delegates to the State convention.

Lastly, the township committees appoint days for "primary meetings" or "caucuses" to elect delegates to the county conventions.

The township, county, and State conventions having been held, the national convention follows at the appointed time and place. When it meets, it is called to order by the chairman of the national committee, who nominates a temporary chairman of the convention. The convention usually accepts the chairman so nominated.

Committees on credentials, on permanent organization, on rules, and on platform, are then appointed. Each of these committees is composed of one member from each State and territory. The members are appointed by their respective delegations.

The committee on credentials hears and determines the claims of delegates to seats as members of the convention

The committee on permanent organization nominates a permanent chairman and other permanent officers of the convention. The committee on rules reports rules for the government of the convention.

The committee on platform prepares and reports to

the convention a platform. A platform consists of certain principles which the party through its convention professes to believe, and certain promises which the party agrees to perform if its candidates are elected.

After the convention has chosen its permanent chairman, and heard and acted on the reports of its committees, it proceeds to vote by ballot for candidates for president and vice-president.

After the candidates are nominated, the convention appoints a new national committee, and then adjourns.

(Probably no two conventions proceed in exactly the same way, but it is believed that the above description corresponds closely to the general course pursued by national, and also by State conventions.)

THE CONGRESSIONAL DISTRICTS OF ILLINOIS.

First—The first, second, third and fourth wards in Chicago, and the towns of Riverside, Hyde Park, Lake, Lyons, Calumet, Worth, Palos, Lemont, Thornton, Bremen, Orland, Bloom, and Rich, in Cook county.

Second—The fifth, sixth and seventh wards of Chicago, and that part of the eighth ward which lies south of the center of Polk street and of Macalister place.

Third—The ninth, tenth, eleventh, twelfth, thirteenth and fourteenth wards of Chicago, and that part of the eighth ward which lies north of the center of Polk street and of Macalister place.

Fourth—The fifteenth, sixteenth, seventeenth and eighteenth wards of Chicago, and the towns of Lake View, Jefferson, Leyden, Norwood Park, Evanston, Niles, Maine, Elk Grove, Schaumberg, Hanover, New Trier, Northfield, Wheeling, Palatine, Barrington, Cicero, and Proviso, in Cook county.

Fifth—Lake, McHenry, Boone, De Kalb and Kane counties.

Sixth—Winnebago, Stephenson, Jo Daviess, Ogle, and Carroll.

Seventh—Lee, Whiteside, Henry, Bureau and Putnam.

Eighth—La Salle, Kendall, Grundy, Will and Du Page.

Ninth—Kankakee, Iroquois, Ford, Livingston, Woodford, and Marshall.

Tenth—Peoria, Knox, Stark and Fulton.

Eleventh—Rock Island, Mercer, Henderson, Warren, Hancock, McDonough and Schuyler.

Twelfth—Cass, Brown, Adams, Pike, Scott, Greene, Jersey and Calhoun.

Thirteenth—Tazewell, Mason, Menard, Sangamon, Morgan and Christian.

Fourteenth — McLean, DeWitt, Piatt, Macon and Logan.

Fifteenth—Coles, Edgar, Douglass, Vermilion and Champaign.

Sixteenth—Cumberland, Clark, Jasper, Crawford, Clay, Richland, Lawrence, Wayne, Edwards and Wabash.

Seventeenth—Macoupin, Montgomery, Shelby, Moultrie, Effingham and Fayette.

Eighteenth—Bond, Madison, St. Clair, Monroe and Washington.

Nineteenth—Marion, Clinton, Jefferson, Franklin, Hamilton, White, Saline, Gallatin and Hardin.

Twentieth—Perry, Randolph, Jackson, Williamson, Union, Johnson, Pope, Alexander, Pulaski and Massac.

SENATORIAL DISTRICTS.

First—The ninth and tenth wards of Chicago, and that part of the eleventh ward north of the center line of Van Buren street.

Second—That part of the fourth ward of Chicago south of the center line of Twenty-ninth street, and the towns of Hyde Park and Lake, in Cook county.

Third—The first, second and third wards of Chicago, and that part of the fourth ward north of the center line of Twenty-ninth street.

Fourth—That part of the eighth ward north of the center line of Taylor street, and that part of the eleventh ward south of the center line of Van Buren street and the twelfth ward of Chicago.

Fifth—That part of the sixth ward west of the center line of Throop street, the seventh ward, and that part of the eighth ward south of the center line of Taylor street, in Chicago.

· Sixth—The eighteenth ward, that part of the sixteenth ward east of the center line of Sedgwick street, and the fifteenth ward of Chicago, and the towns of Lake View and Evanston, in Cook county.

Seventh—The towns of New Trier, Northfield, Wheeling, Palatine, Barrington, Hanover, Schaumberg, Elk Grove, Maine, Niles, Jefferson, Norwood Park, Leyden, Proviso, Cicero, Riverside, Lyons, Lemont, Palos, Worth, Calumet, Thornton, Bremen, Orland, Rich and Bloom, in Cook county.

Eighth—Lake, McHenry and Boone counties.

Ninth—The thirteenth ward, and all of the fourteenth ward except that portion thereof lying east of a line drawn from a point where the center line of Milwaukee avenue intersects the center line of Ohio street, northwest along said center line of Milwaukee avenue to the center line of Ashland avenue, thence north along the center line of Ashland avenue to the center line of Clybourne place, thence northeasterly along the center line of Clybourne place to the north branch of Chicago river, in the city of Chicago.

Tenth—The counties of Winnebago and Ogle.

Eleventh—The fifth ward and that part of the sixth ward east of the center line of Throop street, in Chicago.

Twelfth—Jo Daviess, Stephenson and Carroll counties.

Thirteenth—That part of the fourteenth ward lying east of a line drawn from the intersection of the center line of Milwaukee avenue with the center line of Ohio street, northwest along the center line of said Milwaukee avenue to the center of Ashland avenue, thence north along the center line of Ashland avenue to the center line of Clybourne place, thence northeasterly along the center line of Clybourne place to the north branch of the Chicago river; that part of the sixteenth ward west of the center line of Sedgwick street, and the seventeenth ward, in the city of Chicago.

Fourteenth—Kane and Du Page counties.

Fifteenth—Will.

Sixteenth—Kankakee and Iroquois.

Seventeenth—De Kalb, Kendall and Grundy.

Eighteenth—Livingston and Ford.

Nineteenth—Whiteside and Lee.

Twentieth—Marshall, Woodford and Tazewell.

Twenty-first—Rock Island and Henry.

Twenty-second—Knox and Fulton.

Twenty-third—La Salle.

Twenty-fourth—Hancock, Henderson and Mercer.

Twenty-fifth—Bureau, Stark and Putnam.
Twenty-sixth—Peoria county.
Twenty-seventh—Warren and McDonough.
Twenty-eighth—McLean.
Twenty-ninth—Logan and Macon.
Thirtieth—Champaign, Piatt and De Witt.
Thirty-first—Vermilion and Edgar.
Thirty-second—Douglass, Coles and Cumberland.
Thirty-third—Moultrie, Shelby and Effingham.
Thirty-fourth—Mason, Menard, Cass and Schuyler.
Thirty-fifth—Adams.
Thirty-sixth—Brown, Pike and Calhoun.
Thirty-seventh—Scott, Greene and Jersey.
Thirty-eighth—Macoupin and Morgan.
Thirty-ninth—Sangamon.
Fortieth—Christian and Montgomery.
Forty-first—Madison.
Forty-second—Bond, Clinton and Washington.
Forty-third—Fayette, Marion and Jefferson.
Forty-fourth—Clay, Richland, Wayne and Edwards.
Forty-fifth—Clark, Jasper and Crawford.
Forty-sixth—Hamilton, White, Wabash and Lawrence.
Forty-seventh—St. Clair.
Forty-eighth—Monroe, Randolph and Perry.
Forty-ninth—Saline, Gallatin, Hardin, Pope and Massac.
Fiftieth—Jackson, Union and Alexander.
Fifty-first—Franklin, Williamson, Johnson and Pulaski.

GRAND DIVISIONS OF THE SUPREME COURT.

Southern Grand Division—Terms held at Mount Vernon.

Counties of Alexander, Bond, Clay, Clinton, Crawford, Edwards, Effingham, Fayette, Franklin, Gallatin, Hamilton, Hardin. Jackson, Jasper, Jefferson, Johnson, Lawrence, Madison, Marion, Massac, Monroe, Perry, Pope, Pulaski, Randolph. Richland Saline, St. Clair, Union, Wabash, Washington, Wayne, White and Williamson.

Central Grand Division—Terms held at Springfield.

Counties of Adams, Brown, Cass, Calhoun, Champaign, Christian, Clark, Coles, Cumberland, De Witt, Douglas, Edgar, Ford, Fulton, Greene, Hancock. Jersey, Logan, Macon, Macoupin, Mason, McDonough, McLean, Menard, Montgomery, Morgan, Moultrie, Piatt, Pike, Sangamon, Schuyler, Scott, Shelby, Tazewell and Vermilion.

Northern Grand Division—Terms held at Ottawa.

Counties of Boone, Bureau, Carroll, Cook. De Kalb, Du Page, Grundy, Henderson, Henry. Iroquois, Jo Daviess, Kane, Kankakee, Kendall, Knox, Lake, La Salle, Lee, Livingstone, Marshall, McHenry, Mercer, Ogle, Peoria, Putnam. Rock Island, Stark. Stephenson, Warren, Whiteside, Will, Winnebago and Woodford.

ELECTION DISTRICTS OF SUPREME COURT.

First District—The counties of St Clair, Clinton. Washington, Jefferson. Wayne, Edwards, Wabash, White, Hamilton, Franklin, Perry. Randolph, Monroe, Jackson, Williamson, Saline, Gallatin, Hardin. Pope, Union, Johnson. Alexander. Pulaski and Massac.

Second District — The counties of Madison, Bond, Marion. Clay, Richland, Lawrence, Crawford, Jasper, Effingham, Fayette, Montgomery, Macoupin, Shelby, Cumberland, Clark, Greene, Jersey, Calhoun and Christian.

Third District—The counties of Sangamon, Macon, Logan, De Witt, Piatt, Douglas, Champaign, Vermillion, McLean, Livingston, Ford, Iroquois, Coles, Edgar, Moultrie and Tazewell.

Fourth District—The counties of Fulton, McDonough, Hancock, Schuyler, Brown, Adams, Pike, Mason, Menard, Morgan, Cass and Scott.

Fifth District—The counties of Knox, Warren, Henderson, Mercer, Henry, Stark, Peoria, Marshall, Putnam, Bureau, La Salle, Grundy and Woodford.

Sixth District—The counties of Whiteside, Carroll, Jo Daviess, Stephenson, Winnebago, Boone, McHenry, Kane, Kendall, De Kalb, Lee, Ogle and Rock Island.

Seventh District—The counties of Lake, Cook, Will, Kankakee and Du Page.

APPELLATE COURT DISTRICTS.

First District—Cook county.

Second District—It includes the counties embraced in the northern grand division of the supreme court, except Cook county.

Third District—It includes the counties embraced within the central grand division of the supreme court.

Fourth District—It includes the counties embraced within the southern grand division of the supreme court.

CIRCUIT COURTS.

First Circuit—The counties of Franklin, Saline, Williamson, Jackson, Union, Johnson, Pope, Hardin, Massac, Pulaski and Alexander.

Second Circuit—The counties of Cumberland, Effingham, Clay, Jasper, Richland, Lawrence, Crawford, Jefferson, Wayne, Edwards, Wabash, White, Hamilton and Gallatin.

Third Circuit—The counties of Bond, Madison, St. Clair, Marion, Clinton, Washington, Randolph, Monroe and Perry.

Fourth Circuit—The counties of Vermilion, Edgar, Clark, Coles, Douglas, Champaign, Piatt, Moultrie and Macon.

Fifth Circuit—The counties of Sangamon, Macoupin, Christian, Montgomery, Fayette and Shelby.

Sixth Circuit—The counties of Hancock, Adams, Fulton, McDonough, Schuyler, Brown and Pike.

Seventh Circuit—The counties of De Witt, Logan, Menard, Mason, Cass, Morgan, Scott, Greene, Jersey and Calhoun

Eighth Circuit—The counties of Putnam, Marshall, Woodford, Tazewell, Peoria and Stark.

Ninth Circuit—The counties of Bureau, La Salle, Will and Grundy.

Tenth Circuit—The counties of Rock Island, Mercer, Henry, Henderson, Warren and Knox.

Eleventh Circuit—The counties of McLean, Ford, Kankakee, Iroquois and Livingston.

Twelfth Circuit—The counties of Boone, De Kalb, McHenry, Lake, Kane, Du Page and Kendall.

Thirteenth Circuit—The counties of Jo Daviess, Stephenson, Winnebago, Carroll, Whiteside, Ogle and Lee.

Cook county alone constitutes another circuit.

CONSTITUTION OF THE STATE OF ILLINOIS.

PREAMBLE.

We, the people of the State of Illinois—grateful to Almighty God for the civil, political and religious liberty which He hath so long permitted us to enjoy, and looking to Him for a blessing upon our endeavors to secure and transmit the same unimpaired to succeeding generations—in order to form a more perfect government, establish justice, insure domestic tranquility, provide for the common defense, promote the general welfare, and secure the blessings of liberty to ourselves and our posterity; do ordain and establish this constitution for the State of Illinois.

ARTICLE I.—BOUNDARIES.

The boundaries and jurisdiction of the State shall be as follows, to wit : Beginning at the mouth of the Wabash river ; thence up the same, and with the line of Indiana, to the northwest corner of said State ; thence east, with the line of the same State, to the middle of Lake Michigan; thence north, along the middle of said lake, to north latitude 42 degrees and 30 minutes; thence west to the middle of the Mississippi river, and thence down along the middle of that river to its confluence with the Ohio river, and thence up the latter river, along its northwestern shore, to the place of beginning: *Provided*, that this State shall exercise such jurisdiction upon the Ohio river as she is now entitled to, or such as may hereafter be agreed upon by this State and the State of Kentucky.

ARTICLE II.—BILL OF RIGHTS.

§ 1. All men are by nature free and independent, and have certain inherent and inalienable rights—among these are life, liberty and the pursuit of happiness. To secure these rights and the protection of property, governments are instituted among men, deriving their just powers from the consent of the governed.

§ 2. No person shall be deprived of life, liberty or property, without due process of law.

§ 3. The free exercise and enjoyment of religious profession and worship, without discrimination, shall forever be guaranteed ; and no person shall be denied any civil or political right, privilege or capacity, on account of his religious opinions ; but the liberty of conscience hereby secured shall not be construed to dispense with oaths or affirmations, excuse acts of licentiousness, or justify practices inconsistent with the peace or safety of the State. No person shall be required to attend or support any ministry or place of worship against his consent, nor shall any preference be given by law to any religious denomination or mode of worship.

§ 4. Every person may freely speak, write and publish on all subjects, being responsible for the abuse of that liberty; and in all trials for libel, both civil and criminal, the truth, when published with good motives and for justifiable ends, shall be a sufficient defense.

§ 5 The right of trial by jury as heretofore enjoyed, shall remain inviolate; but the trial of civil cases before justices of the peace by a jury of less than twelve men, may be authorized by law.

§ 6. The right of the people to be secure in their persons, houses, papers, and effects, against unreasonable searches and seizures, shall not be violated; and no warrant shall issue without probable cause, supported by affidavit, particularly describing the place to be searched, and the person or things to be seized.

§ 7. All persons shall be bailable by sufficient sureties, except for capital offenses, where the proof is evident or the presumption great; and the privilege of the writ of *habeas corpus* shall not be suspended, unless when in cases of rebellion or invasion the public safety may require it.

§ 8. No person shall be held to answer for a criminal offense unless on indictment of a grand jury, except in cases in which the punishment is by fine, or imprisonment otherwise than in the penitentiary, in cases of impeachment, and in cases arising in the army and navy or in the militia when in actual service in time of war or public danger: *Provided*, that the grand jury may be abolished by law in all cases.

§ 9. In all criminal prosecutions, the accused shall have the right to appear and defend in person and by counsel; to demand the nature and cause of the accusation, and to have a copy thereof; to meet the witnesses face to face, and to have process to compel the attendance of witnesses in his behalf, and a speedy public trial by an impartial jury of the county or district in which the offense is alleged to have been committed.

§ 10. No person shall be compelled in any criminal case to give evidence against himself, or be twice put in jeopardy for the same offense.

§ 11. All penalties shall be proportioned to the nature of the offense: and no conviction shall work corruption of blood or forfeiture of estate; nor shall any person be transported out of the State for any offense committed within the same.

§ 12. No person shall be imprisoned for debt, unless upon refusal to deliver up his estate for the benefit of his creditors, in such manner as shall be prescribed by law ; or in cases where there is strong presumption of fraud.

§ 13. Private property shall not be taken or damaged for public use without just compensation. Such compensation, when not made by the State, shall be ascertained by a jury, as shall be prescribed by law. The fee of land taken for railroad tracks without consent of the owners thereof, shall remain in such owners, subject to the use for which it is taken.

§ 14. No *ex post facto* law, or law impairing the obligation of contracts, or making any irrevocable grant of special privileges or immunities, shall be passed.

§ 15. The military shall be in strict subordination to the civil power.

§ 16. No soldier shall, in time of peace, be quartered in any house without the consent of the owner; nor in time of war except in the manner prescribed by law.

§ 17. The people have the right to assemble in a peaceable manner to consult for the common good, to make known their opinions to their representatives, and to apply for redress of grievances.

§ 18. All elections shall be free and equal.

§ 19. Every person ought to find a certain remedy in the laws for all injuries and wrongs which he may receive in his person, property, or reputation; he ought to obtain, by law, right and justice freely, and without being obliged to purchase it, completely and without denial, promptly and without delay.

§ 20. A frequent recurrence to the fundamental principles of civil government is absolutely necessary to preserve the blessings of liberty.

ARTICLE III.—DISTRIBUTION OF POWERS.

The powers of the government of this State are divided into three distinct departments—the legislative, executive and judicial; and no person, or collection of persons, being one of these departments, shall exercise any power properly belonging to either of the others, except as hereinafter expressly directed or permitted.

ARTICLE IV.—LEGISLATIVE DEPARTMENT.

§ 1. The legislative power shall be vested in a general assembly, which shall consist of a senate and house of representatives, both to be elected by the people.

ELECTION.

§ 2. An election for members of the general assembly shall be held on the Tuesday next after the first Monday in November in the year of our Lord one thousand eight hundred and seventy, and every two years thereafter, in each county, at such places therein as may be provided by law. When vacancies occur in either house, the governor or person exercising the powers of governor, shall issue writs of election to fill such vacancies.

ELIGIBILITY AND OATH.

§ 3. No person shall be a senator who shall not have attained the age of twenty-five years, or a representative who shall not have attained the age of twenty-one years. No person shall be a senator or a representative who shall not be a citizen of the United States, and who shall not have been for five years a resident of this State, and for two years next preceding his election a resident within the territory forming the district from which he is elected. No judge or clerk of any court; secretary of state, attorney-general, state's attorney, recorder, sheriff, or collector of public revenue, member of either house of congress, or person holding any lucrative office under the United States or this State, or any foreign government, shall have a seat in the general assembly: *Provided*, that appointments in the militia, and the offices of notary public and justice of the peace shall not be considered lucrative. Nor shall any person, holding any office of honor or profit under any foreign government, or under the government of the United States (except post-masters whose annual compensation does not exceed the sum of $300), hold any office of honor or profit under the authority of this State.

§ 4. No person who has been, or hereafter shall be, convicted of bribery, perjury or other infamous crime, nor any person who has been or may be a collector or holder of public moneys, who shall not have accounted for and paid over, according to law, all such moneys due from him, shall be eligible to the general assembly, or to any office of profit or trust in this State.

§ 5. Members of the general assembly, before they enter upon their official duties, shall take and subscribe to the following oath or affirmation.

" I do solemnly swear (or affirm) that I will support the constitution of the United States, and the constitution of the State of Illinois, and will faithfully discharge the duties of senator (or representative) according to the best of my ability; and that I have not, knowingly or intentionally, paid or contributed anything, or made any promise in the nature of a bribe, to directly or indirectly influence any vote at the election at which I was chosen to fill the said office, and have not accepted, nor will I accept or receive, directly or indirectly, any money or other valuable thing. from any corporation. company or person, for any vote or influence I may give or withhold on any bill, resolution or appropriation, or for any other official act."

This oath shall be administered by a judge of the supreme or circuit court, in the hall of the house to which the member is elected, and the secretary of state shall record and file the oath subscribed by each member. Any member who shall refuse to take the oath herein prescribed, shall forfeit his office, and every member who shall be convicted of having sworn falsely to, or of violating, his said oath, shall forfeit his office, and be disqualified thereafter from holding any office of profit or trust in this State.

APPORTIONMENT—SENATORIAL.

§ 6. The general assembly shall apportion the State every 10 years, beginning with the year 1871, by dividing the population of the State, as ascertained by the federal census, by the number 51, and the quotient shall be the ratio of representation in the senate. The State shall be divided into 51 senatorial districts each of which shall elect one senator, whose term of office shall be four years. The senators elected in the year of our Lord 1872, in districts bearing odd numbers, shall vacate their offices at the end of two years, and those elected in districts bearing even numbers, at the end of four years; and vacancies occurring by the expiration of term, shall be filled by the election of senators for the full term. Senatorial districts shall be formed of contiguous and compact territory, bounded by county lines, and contain as nearly as practicable an equal number of inhabitants; but no district shall contain less than four-fifths of the senatorial ratio. Counties containing not less than the ratio and three-fourths, may be divided into separate districts, and shall be entitled to two senators, and to one additional senator for each number of inhabitants equal to the ratio, contained in such counties in excess of twice the number of said ratio.

NOTE.—By the adoption of minority representation, §§ 7 and 8, of this article, cease to be a part of the constitution. Under § 12 of the schedule, and the vote of adoption, the following section relating to minority representation is substituted for said sections:

MINORITY REPRESENTATION.

§§ 7 and 8. The house of representatives shall consist of three times the number of the members of the senate, and the term of office shall be two years. Three representatives shall be elected in each senatorial district at the general election in the year of our Lord 1872, and every two years thereafter. In all elections of representatives aforesaid, each qualified voter may cast as many votes for one candidate as there are representatives to be elected, or may distribute the same, or equal parts thereof, among the candidates, as he shall see fit; and the candidates highest in votes shall be declared elected.

TIME OF MEETING AND GENERAL RULES.

§ 9. The sessions of the general assembly shall commence at 12 o'clock noon, on the Wednesday next after the first Monday in January, in the year next ensuing the election of members thereof, and at no other time, unless as provided by this constitution. A majority of the members elected to each house shall constitute a quorum. Each house shall determine the rules of its proceedings, and be the judge of the election, returns and qualifications of its members; shall choose its own officers; and the senate shall choose a temporary president to preside when the lieutenant-governor shall not attend as president or shall act as governor. The secretary of state shall call the house of representatives to order at the opening of each new assembly, and preside over it until a temporary presiding officer thereof shall have been chosen and shall have taken his seat. No member shall be expelled by either house, except by a vote of two-thirds of all the members elected to that house, and no member shall be twice expelled for the same offense. Each house may punish by imprisonment any person, not a member, who shall be guilty of disrespect to the house by disorderly or contemptuous behavior in its presence. But no such imprisonment shall extend beyond 24 hours at one time, unless the person shall persist in such disorderly or contemptuous behavior.

§ 10. The doors of each house and of committees of the whole shall be kept open, except in such cases as, in the opinion of the house, require secrecy. Neither house shall, without the consent of the other, adjourn for more than two days, or to any other place than that in which the two houses shall be sitting. Each house shall keep a journal of its proceedings, which shall be published. In the senate at the request of two members, and in the house at the request of five members, the yeas and nays shall be taken on any question, and entered upon the journal. Any two members of either house shall have liberty to dissent from and protest, in respectful language, against any act or resolution which they think injurious to the public or to any individual, and have the reasons of their dissent entered upon the journals.

STYLE OF LAWS AND PASSAGE OF BILLS.

§ 11. The style of the laws of this State shall be: *Be it enacted by the People of the State of Illinois, represented in the General Assembly.*

§ 12. Bills may originate in either house, but may be altered, amended or rejected by the other; and on the final passage of all bills, the vote shall be by yeas and nays, upon each bill separately, and shall be entered upon the journal; and no bill shall become a law without the concurrence of a majority of the members elected to each house.

§ 13. Every bill shall be read at large on three different days, in each house; and the bill and all amendments thereto, shall be printed before the vote is taken on its final passage; and every bill, having passed both houses, shall be signed by the speakers thereof No act hereafter passed shall embrace more than one subject, and that shall be expressed in the title. But if any subject shall be embraced in an act which shall not be expressed in the title, such act shall be void only as to so much thereof as shall not be so expressed; and no law shall be revived or amended by reference to its title only, but the law revived, or the section amended, shall be inserted at length in the new act. And no act of the general assembly shall take effect until the first day of July next after its passage, unless, in case of emergency, (which emergency shall be expressed in the preamble or body of the act), the general assembly shall, by a vote of two-thirds of all the members elected to each house, otherwise direct.

PRIVILEGES AND DISABILITIES.

§ 14. Senators and representatives shall, in all cases, except treason, felony or breach of the peace, be privileged from arrest during the session of the general assembly, and in going to and returning from the same; and for any speech or debate in either house, they shall not be questioned in any other place.

§ 15. No person elected to the general assembly shall receive any civil appointment within this State from the governor, the governor and senate, or from the general assembly, during the term for which he shall have been elected; and all such appointments, and all votes given for any such members for any such office or appointment, shall be void; nor shall any member of the general assembly be interested, either directly or indirectly, in any contract with the State, or any county thereof, authorized by any law passed during the term for which he shall have been elected, or within one year after the expiration thereof.

PUBLIC MONEYS AND APPROPRIATIONS.

§ 16. The general assembly shall make no appropriation of money out of the treasury in any private law. Bills making appropriations for the pay of members and officers of the general assembly, and for the salaries of the officers of the government, shall contain no provisions on any other subject.

§ 17. No money shall be drawn from the treasury except in pursuance of an appropriation made by law, and on the presentation of a warrant issued by the auditor thereon: and no money shall be diverted from any appropriation made for any purpose, or taken from any fund whatever, either by joint or separate resolution. The auditor shall, within 60 days after the adjournment of each session of the general assembly, prepare and publish a full statement of all money expended at such session, specifying the amount of each item, and to whom and for what paid.

§ 18. Each general assembly shall provide for all the appropriations necessary for the ordinary and contingent expenses of the government until the expiration of the first fiscal quarter after the adjournment of the next regular session, the aggregate amount of which shall not be increased without a vote of two-thirds of the members elected to each house, nor exceed the amount of revenue authorized by law to be raised in such time; and all appropriations, general or special, requiring money to be paid out of the State Treasury, from funds belonging to the State, shall end with such fiscal quarter: *Provided*, the State may, to meet casual deficits or failures in revenues, contract debts, never to exceed in the aggregate $250,000; and moneys thus borrowed shall be applied to the purpose for which they were obtained, or to pay the debt thus created, and to no other purpose; and no other debt, except for the purpose of repelling invasion, suppressing insurrection, or defending the State in war (for payment of which the faith of the State shall be pledged), shall be contracted, unless the law authorizing the same shall, at a general election, have been submitted to the people, and have received a majority of the votes cast for members of the general assembly at such election. The general assembly shall provide for the publication of said law for three months, at least, before the vote of the people shall be taken upon the same; and provision shall be made, at the time, for the payment of the interest annually, as it shall accrue, by a tax levied for the purpose, or from other sources of revenue;

which law, providing for the payment of such interest by such tax, shall be irrepealable until such debt be paid: *And provided further*, that the law levying the tax shall be submitted to the people with the law authorizing the debt to be contracted.

§ 19. The general assembly shall never grant or authorize extra compensation, fee or allowance to any public officer, agent, servant or contractor, after service has been rendered or a contract made, nor authorize the payment of any claim, or part thereof, hereafter created against the State under any agreement or contract made without express authority of law; and all such unauthorized agreements or contracts shall be null and void. *Provided*, the general assembly may make appropriations for expenditures incurred in suppressing insurrection or repelling invasion.

§ 20. The State shall never pay, assume, or become responsible for the debts or liabilities of, or in any manner give, loan or extend its credit to, or in aid of any public or other corporation, association or individual.

PAY OF MEMBERS.

§ 21. The members of the general assembly shall receive for their services the sum of $5 per day during the first session held under this constitution, and 10 cents for each mile necessarily traveled in going to and returning from the seat of government, to be computed by the auditor of public accounts; and thereafter such compensation as shall be prescribed by law, and no other allowance or emolument, directly or indirectly, for any purpose whatever; except the sum of $50 per session to each member, which shall be in full for postage, stationery, newspapers, and all other incidental expenses and perquisites; but no change shall be made in the compensation of members of the general assembly during the term for which they may have been elected. The pay and mileage allowed to each member of the general assembly shall be certified by the speaker of their respective houses, and entered on the journals and published at the close of each session.

SPECIAL LEGISLATION PROHIBITED.

§ 22. The general assembly shall not pass local or special laws in any of the following enumerated cases, that is to say : for—
Granting divorces;
Changing the names of persons or places;
Laying out, opening, altering, and working roads or highways;
Vacating roads, town plats, streets, alleys and public grounds ;
Locating or changing county seats;

Regulating county and township affairs;

Regulating the practice in courts of justice ;

Regulating the jurisdiction and duties of justices of the peace, police magistrates and constables;

Providing for changes of venue in civil and criminal cases;

Incorporating cities, towns or villages, or changing or amending the charter of any town, city or village;

Providing for the election of members of the board of supervisors in townships, incorporated towns or cities;

Summoning or impaneling grand or petit juries;

Providing for the management of common schools;

Regulating the rate of interest on money ;

The opening and conducting of any election, or designating the place of voting;

The sale or mortgage of real estate belonging to minors or others under disability;

The protection of game or fish;

Chartering or licensing ferries or toll bridges ;

Remitting fines, penalties or forfeitures;

Creating, increasing or decreasing fees, percentage or allowances of public officers during the term for which said officers are elected or appointed;

Changing the law of descent;

Granting to any corporation, association or individual the right to lay down railroad tracks, or amending existing charters for such purpose;

Granting to any corporation, association or individual any special or exclusive privilege, immunity or franchise whatever;

In all other cases where a general law can be made applicable, no special law shall be enacted.

§ 23. The general assembly shall have no power to release or extinguish, in whole or in part, the indebtedness, liability, or obligation of any corporation or individual to this state or to any municipal corporation therein.

IMPEACHMENT.

§ 24. The house of representatives shall have the sole power of impeachment; but a majority of all the members elected must concur therein. All impeachments shall be tried by the senate ; and when sitting for that purpose the senators shall be upon oath, or affirmation, to do justice according to law and evidence. When the governor of the State is tried the chief justice shall preside. No person shall be convicted without the concurrence of two thirds of the senators elected   But judgment, in such cases, shall not extend further than removal from office and disqualification to hold any office of honor, profit or trust under the government of this State   The party, whether convicted or acquitted, shall, nevertheless, be liable to prosecution, trial, judgment and punishment according to law.

MISCELLANEOUS.

§ 25.   The general assembly shall provide, by law, that the fuel, stationery, and printing paper furnished for the use of the State; the copying printing, binding and distributing the laws and journals, and all other printing ordered by the general assembly, shall be let by contract to the lowest responsible bidder ; but the general assembly shall fix a maximum price ; and no member thereof, or other officer of the State, shall be interested, directly or indirectly, in such contract.   But all such contracts shall be subject to the approval of the governor, and if he disapproves the same there shall be a re-letting of the contract, in such a manner as shall be prescribed by law.

§ 26.   The State of Illinois shall never be made defendant in any court of law or equity.

§ 27.   The general assembly shall have no power to authorize lotteries or gift enterprises, for any purpose, and shall pass laws to prohibit the sale of lottery or gift enterprise tickets in this State.

§ 28.   No law shall be passed which shall operate to extend the term of any public officer after his election or appointment.

§ 29.   It shall be the duty of the general assembly to pass such laws as may be necessary for the protection of operative miners, by providing for ventilation, when the same may be required, and the construction of escapement shafts or such other appliances as may secure safety in all coal mines, and to provide for the enforcement of said laws by such penalties and punishments as may be deemed proper.

§ 30.   The general assembly may provide for establishing and opening roads and cartways, connected with a public road, for private and public use.

§ 31.   The general assembly may pass laws permitting the owners or occupants of lands to construct drains and ditches, for agricultural and sanitary purposes, across the lands of others.

§ 32.   The general assembly shall pass liberal homestead and exemption laws.

§ 23.   The general assembly shall not appropriate out of the State treasury, or expend on account of the new capitol grounds, and construction, completion, and furnishing of the new State house, a sum exceeding in the aggregate, $3,500,000 inclusive of all appropriations heretofore made, without first submitting the proposition for an additional expenditure to the legal voters of the State, at a general election; nor unless a majority of all the votes cast at such election shall be for the proposed additional expenditure.

ARTICLE V.—EXECUTIVE DEPARTMENT.

§ 1. The executive department shall consist of a Governor, Lieutenant-Governor, Secretary of State, Auditor of Public Accounts, Treasurer, Superintendent of Public Instruction, and Attorney-General, who shall, each with the exception of the Treasurer, hold his office for the term of four years from the second Monday of January next after his election, and until his successor is elected and qualified. They shall, except the Lieutenant-Governor, reside at the seat of government during their term of office, and keep the public records, books and papers there, and shall perform such duties as may be prescribed by law.

§ 2. The Treasurer shall hold his office for the term of two years, and unt l his successor is elected and qualified ; and shall be ineligible to said office for two years next after the end of the term for which he was elected. He may be required by the Governor to give reasonable additional security, and in default of so doing his office shall be deemed vacant.

ELECTION.

§ 3. An election for Governor, Lieutenant-Governor, Secretary of State, Auditor of Public Accounts, and Attorney-General, shall be held on the Tuesday next after the first Monday of November, in the year of our Lord 1872, and every four years thereafter ; for Superintendent of Public Instruction, on the Tuesday next after the first Monday of November, in the year 1870, and every four years thereafter ; and for Treasurer, on the day last above mentioned, and every two years thereafter, at such places and in such manner as may be prescribed by law.

§ 4. The returns of every election for the above-named officers shall be sealed up and transmitted, by the returning officers, to the Secretary of State, directed to " The Speaker of the House of Representatives," who shall, immediately after the organization of the house, and before proceeding to other business, open and publish the same in the presence of a majority of each house of the general assembly, who shall, for that purpose, assemble in the hall of the house of representatives. The person having the highest number of votes for either of said offices shall be declared duly elected ; but if two or more have an equal and the highest number of votes, the general assembly shall, by joint ballot, choose one of such persons for said office. Contested elections for all of said offices shall be determined by both houses of the general assembly, by joint ballot, in such manner as may be prescribed by law.

ELIGIBILITY.

§ 5. No person shall be eligible to the office of governor or lieutenant-governor who shall not have attained the age of 30 years, and been for five years next preceding his election a citizen of the United States and of this State. Neither the governor, lieutenant-governor, auditor of public accounts, secretary of State, superintendent of public instruction, nor attorney-general shall be eligible to any other office during the period for which he shall have been elected.

GOVERNOR.

§ 6. The supreme executive power shall be vested in the governor, who shall take care that the laws be faithfully executed.

§ 7. The governor shall, at the commencement of each session, and at the close of his term of office, give to the general assembly information, by message, of the condition of the State, and shall recommend such measures as he shall deem expedient. He shall account to the general assembly, and accompany his message with a statement of all moneys received and paid out by him from any funds subject to his order, with vouchers, and, at the commencement of each regular session present estimates of the amount of money required to be raised by taxation for all purposes.

§ 8. The governor may, on extraordinary occasions, convene the general assembly, by proclamation, stating therein the purpose for which they are convened ; and the general assembly shall enter upon no business except that for which they were called together.

§ 9. In case of a disagreement between the two houses with respect to the time of adjournment, the governor may, on the same being certified to him, by the house first moving the adjournment, adjourn the general assembly to such time as he thinks proper, not beyond the first day of the next regular session.

§ 10. The governor shall nominate, and by and with the advice and consent of the senate (a majority of all the senators elected concurring by yeas and nays), appoint all officers whose offices are established by this constitution, or which may be created by law, and whose appointment or election is not otherwise provided for ; and no such officer shall be appointed or elected by the general assembly.

§ 11. In case of a vacancy, during the recess of the senate, in any office which is not elective, the governor shall make a temporary appointment until the next meeting of the senate, when he shall nom- inate some person to fill such office ; and any person so nominated, who is confirmed by the senate (a majority of all the senators elected concurring by yeas and nays), shall hold his office during the remain- der of the term, and until his successor shall be appointed and quali- fied. No person, after being rejected by the senate, shall be again nominated for the same office at the same session, unless at the request of the senate, or be appointed to the same office during the recess of the general assembly.

§ 12. The governor shall have power to remove any officer whom he may appoint, in case of incompetency, neglect of duty, or mal- feasance in office ; and he may declare his office vacant, and fill the same as is herein provided in other cases of vacancy.

§ 13. The governor shall have power to grant reprieves, commu- tations and pardons, after conviction, for all offenses subject to such regulations as may be provided by law relative to the manner of ap- plying therefor.

§ 14. The governor shall be commander-in-chief of the military and naval forces of the State (except when they shall be called into the service of the United States) ; and may call out the same to execute the laws, suppress insurrection, and repel invasion.

§ 15. The governor, and all civil officers of this State, shall be liable to impeachment for any misdemeanor in office.

VETO. ◆

§ 16. Every bill passed by the general assembly shall, before it becomes a law, be presented to the governor. If he approve, he shall sign it, and thereupon it shall become a law ; but if he do not approve, he shall return it, with his objections, to the house in which it shall have originated, which house shall enter the objections at large upon its journal, and proceed to reconsider the bill. If, then, two-thirds of the members elected agree to pass the same, it shall be sent to- gether with the objections, to the other house, by which it shall like- wise be reconsidered ; and if approved by two-thirds of the members elected to that house, it shall become a law, notwithstanding the objections of the governor. But in all such cases the vote of each house shall be determined by yeas and nays, to be entered on the journal. Any bill which shall not be returned by the governor within ten days (Sundays excepted) after it shall have been presented to him, shall become a law in like manner as if he had signed it, unless the general assembly shall, by their adjournment, prevent its return ; in which case it shall be filed, with his objections, in the office of the secretary of State, within ten days after such adjournment, or become a law.

LIEUTENANT GOVERNOR.

§ 17. In case of death, conviction on impeachment, failure to qualify, resignation, absence from the State, or other disability of the governor, the powers, duties and emoluments of the office for the residue of the term, or until the disability shall be removed, shall devolve upon the lieutenant-governor.

§ 18. The lieutenant-governor shall be president of the senate, and shall vote only when the senate is equally divided. The senate shall choose a president, *pro tempore*, to preside in case of the absence or impeachment of the lieutenant-governor, or when he shall hold the office of governor.

§ 19. If there be no lieutenant-governor, or if the lieutenant-governor shall, for any of the causes specified in § 17 of this article, become incapable of performing the duties of the office, the president of the senate shall act as governor until the vacancy is filled or the disability removed ; and if the president of the senate, for any of the above named causes, shall become incapable of performing the duties of governor, the same shall devolve upon the speaker of the house of representatives.

OTHER STATE OFFICERS.

§ 20. If the office of auditor of public accounts, treasurer, secretary of State, attorney-general, or superintendent of public instruction shall be vacated by death, resignation or otherwise, it shall be the duty of the governor to fill the same by appointment, and the appointee shall hold his office until his successor shall be elected and qualified in such manner as may be provided by law. An account shall be kept by the officers of the executive department, and of all the public institutions of the State, of all moneys received or disbursed by them, severally, from all sources, and for every service performed, and a semi-annual report thereof be made to the governor, under oath ; and any officer who makes a false report shall be guilty of perjury, and punished accordingly.

§ 21. The officers of the executive department, and of all the public institutions of the State, shall, at least ten days preceding each regular session of the general assembly, severally report to the governor, who shall transmit such reports to the general assembly, together with the reports of the judges of the supreme court of the defects in the constitution and laws; and the governor may at any time require information, in writing, under oath, from the officers of the executive department, and all officers and managers of State institutions, upon any subject relating to the condition, management and expenses of their respective offices.

THE SEAL OF STATE.

§ 22. There shall be a seal of the State, which shall be called the "Great Seal of the State of Illinois," which shall be kept by the secretary of State, and used by him, officially, as directed by law.

FEES AND SALARIES.

§ 23. The officers named in this article shall receive for their services a salary, to be established by law, which shall not be increased or diminished during their official terms, and they shall not, after the expiration of the terms of those in office at the adoption of this constitution, receive to their own use any fees, costs, perquisites of office, or other compensation. And all fees that may hereafter be payable by law for any service performed by any officer provided for in this article of the constitution, shall be paid in advance into the State treasury.

DEFINITION AND OATH OF OFFICE.

§ 24. An office is a public position created by the constitution or law, continuing during the pleasure of the appointing power, or for a fixed time, with a successor elected or appointed. An employment is an agency, for a temporary purpose, which ceases when that purpose is accomplished.

§ 25. All civil officers, except members of the general assembly, and such inferior officers as may be by law exempted, shall, before they enter on the duties of their respective offices, take and subscribe the following oath or affirmation:

"I do solemnly swear (or affirm, as the case may be) that I will support the constitution of the United States, and the constitution of the State of Illinois, and that I will faithfully discharge the duties of the office of —— according to the best of my ability."

And no other oath, declaration or test shall be required as a qualification.

ARTICLE VI.—JUDICIAL DEPARTMENT.

§ 1. The Judicial powers, except as in this article is otherwise provided, shall be vested in one supreme court, circuit courts, county courts, justices of the peace, police magistrates, and in such courts as may be created by law in and for cities and incorporated towns.

SUPREME COURT.

§ 2. The supreme court shall consist of seven judges, and shall have original jurisdiction in cases relating to the revenue, in *mandamus* and *habeas corpus*, and appellate jurisdiction in all other cases. One of said judges shall be chief justice; four shall constitute a quorum, and the concurrence of four shall be necessary to every decision.

§ 3. No person shall be eligible to the office of judge of the supreme court unless he shall be at least 30 years of age, and a citizen of the United States, nor unless he shall have resided in this State five years next preceding his election, and be a resident of the district in which he shall be elected.

§ 4. Terms of the supreme court shall continue to be held in the present grand divisions at the several places now provided for holding the same; and until otherwise provided by law, one or more terms of said court shall be held, for the northern division, in the city of Chicago, each year, at such times as said court may appoint, whenever said city or the county of Cook shall provide appropriate rooms therefor, and the use of a suitable library, without expense to the State. The judicial divisions may be altered, increased or diminished in number, and the times and places of holding said court m iy be changed by law.

§ 5. The present grand divisions shall be preserved, and be denominated Southern, Central and Northern, until otherwise provided by law. The State shall be divided into seven districts for the election of judges, and, until otherwise provided by law, they shall be as follows:

First District.—The counties of St. Clair, Clinton, Washington, Jefferson, Wayne, Edwards, Wabash. White, Hamilton, Franklin, Perry, Randolph. Monroe, Jackson, Williamson, Saline, Gallatin, Hardin, Pope, Union. Johnson, Alexander, Pulaski and Massac.

Second District.—The counties of Madison, Bond, Marion, Clay, Richland, Lawrence, Crawford, Jasper, Effingham, Fayette. Montgomery, Macoupin, Shelby, Cumberland, Clark, Greene, Jersey, Calhoun and Christian.

Third District.—The counties of Sangamon, Macon, Logan, De

Witt, Piatt, Douglas, Champaign, Vermillion, McLean, Livingston, Ford, Iroquois, Coles, Edgar, Moultrie and Tazewell.

Fourth District.—The counties of Fulton, McDonough, Hancock, Schuyler, Brown, Adams, Pike, Mason, Menard, Morgan, Cass and Scott.

Fifth District.—The counties of Knox, Warren, Henderson, Mercer, Henry, Stark, Peoria, Marshall, Putnam, Bureau, La Salle, Grundy and Woodford.

Sixth District.—The counties of Whiteside, Carroll, Jo Daviess, Stephenson, Winnebago, Boone, McHenry, Kane, Kendall, De Kalb, Lee, Ogle and Rock Island.

Seventh District.—The counties of Lake, Cook, Will, Kankakee and Du Page.

The boundaries of the districts may be changed at the session of the general assembly next preceding the election for judges therein, and at no other time; but whenever such alteration shall be made, the same shall be upon the rule of equality of population, as nearly as county boundaries will allow, and the districts shall be composed of contiguous counties, in as nearly compact form as circumstances will permit. The alteration of the districts shall not affect the tenure of office of any judge.

§ 6. At the time of voting on the adoption of this constitution, one judge of the supreme court shall be elected by the electors thereof, in each of said districts numbered two, three, six and seven, who shall hold his office for the term of nine years from the first Monday of June, in the year of our Lord 1870. The term of office of judges of the supreme court, elected after the adoption of this constitution, shall be nine years; and on the first Monday of June of the year in which the term of any of the judges in office at the adoption of this constitution, or of the judges then elected, shall expire, and every nine years thereafter, there shall be an election for the successor or successors of such judges, in the respective districts wherein the term of such judges shall expire. The chief justice shall continue to act as such until the expiration of the term for which he was elected, after which the judges shall choose one of their number chief justice.

§ 7. From and after the adoption of this constitution, the judges of the supreme court shall each receive a salary of $4,000 per annum, payable quarterly, until otherwise provided by law. And after said salaries shall be fixed by law, the salaries of the judges in office shall not be increased or diminished during the terms for which said judges have been elected.

§ 8. Appeals and writs of error may be taken to the supreme court held in the grand division in which the case is decided, or, by consent of the parties, to any other grand division.

§ 9. The supreme court shall appoint one reporter of its decis-ions, who shall hold his office for six years, subject to removal by the court.

§ 10. At the time of the election for representatives in the general assembly, happening next preceding the expiration of the terms of office of the present clerks of said court, one clerk of said court for each division shall be elected, whose term of office shall be for six years from said election, but who shall not enter upon the duties of his office until the expiration of the term of his predecessor, and every six years thereafter one clerk of said court for each division shall be elected.

APPELLATE COURTS.

§ 11. After the year of our Lord 1874, inferior appellate courts, of uniform organization and jurisdiction, may be created in districts formed for that purpose, to which such appeals and writs of error as the general assembly may provide may be prosecuted from circuit and other courts, and from which appeals and writs of error shall lie to the supreme court, in all criminal cases, and cases in which a fran-chise, or freehold, or the validity of a statute is involved, and in such other cases as may be provided by law. Such appellate courts shall be held by such number of judges of the circuit courts, and at such times and places, and in such manner, as may be provided by law ; but no judge shall sit in review upon cases decided by him ; nor shall said judges receive any additional compensation for such services.

CIRCUIT COURTS.

§ 12. The circuit courts shall have original jurisdiction of all causes in law and equity, and such appellate jurisdiction as is or may be provided by law, and shall hold two or more terms each year in every county. The terms of office of judges of circuit courts shall be six years.

§ 13. The State, exclusive of the county of Cook and other counties having a population of 100,000, shall be divided into judi-cial circuits prior to the expiration of the terms of office of the present judges of the circuit courts. Such circuits shall be formed of contiguous counties, in as nearly compact form and as nearly equal as circumstances will permit, having due regard to business, territory and population, and shall not exceed in number one circuit for every 100,000 of population in the State. One judge shall be elected for each of said circuits by the electors thereof. New circuits may be formed and the boundaries of circuits changed by the general assembly, at its session next preceding the election for circuits judges, but at no other time ; *Provided*, that the circuits may be equalized or changed at the first session of the general assembly after the adoption of this constitution. The creation, alteration or change of any circuit shall not affect the tenure of office of any judge. Whenever the business of the circuit court of any one, or of two or more contiguous counties, containing a population exceeding 50,000, shall occupy nine months of the year, the general assembly may make of such county or counties a separate circuit. Whenever additional circuits are created, the foregoing limitations shall be observed.

§ 14. The general assembly shall provide for the times of holding court in each county, which shall not be changed, except by the general assembly next preceding the general election for judges of said courts ; but additional terms may be provided for in any county. The election for judges of the circuit courts shall be held on the first Monday in June, in the year of our Lord 1873, and every six years thereafter.

§ 15. The general assembly may divide the State into judicial circuits of greater population and territory, in lieu of the circuits provided for in section 13 of this article, and provide for the election therein, severally, by the electors thereof, by general ticket, of not exceeding four judges, who shall hold the circuit courts in the circuits for which they shall be elected, in such manner as may be provided by law.

§ 16. From and after the adoption of this constitution, judges of the circuit courts shall receive a salary of $3,000 per annum, payable quarterly, until otherwise provided by law. And after their salaries shall be fixed by law, they shall not be increased or diminished during the terms for which said judges shall be, respectively, elected ; and from and after the adoption of this constitution, no judge of the supreme or circuit court shall receive any other compensation, perquisite or benefit, in any form whatsoever, nor perform any other than judicial duties to which may belong any emoluments.

§ 17. No person shall be eligible to the office of judge of the circuit or any inferior court, or to membership in the "board of county commissioners," unless he shall be at least 25 years of age, and a citizen of the United States, nor unless he shall have resided in this State five years next preceding his election, and be a resident of the circuit, county, city, cities, or incorporated town in which he shall be elected.

COUNTY COURTS.

§ 18. There shall be elected in and for each county, one county judge and one clerk of the county court, whose terms of office shall be four years. But the general assembly may create districts of two or more contiguous counties, in each of which shall be elected one judge, who shall take the place of, and exercise the powers and juris-diction of county judges in such districts. County courts shall be courts of record, and shall have original jurisdiction in all matters of probate ; settlement of estates of deceased persons ; appointment of guardians and conservators, and settlements of their accounts ; in all matters relating to apprentices, and in proceedings for the collection of taxes and assessments, and such other jurisdiction as may be pro-vided for by general law.

§ 19. Appeals and writs of error shall be allowed from final determinations of county courts, as may be provided by law.

PROBATE COURTS.

§ 20. The general assembly may provide for the establishment of a probate court in each county having a population of over 50,000, and for the election of a judge thereof, whose term of office shall be the same as that of the county judge, and who shall be elected at the same time and in the same manner. Said courts, when established, shall have original jurisdiction of all probate matters, the settlement of estates of deceased persons, the appointment of guardians, con-servators, and settlement of their accounts ; in all matters relating to apprentices, and in cases of the sales of real estate of deceased per-sons for the payment of debts.

JUSTICES OF THE PEACE AND CONSTABLES.

§ 21. Justices of the peace, police magistrates, and constables shall be elected in and for such districts as are, or may be, provided by law, and the jurisdiction of such justices of the peace and police magistrates shall be uniform.

STATE'S ATTORNEYS.

§ 22. At the election for members of the general assembly in the year of our Lord 1872, and every four years thereafter, there shall be elected a State's attorney in and for each county, in lieu of the State's attorneys now provided by law, whose term of office shall be four years.

COURTS OF COOK COUNTY.

§ 23. The county of Cook shall be one judicial circuit. The circuit court of Cook county shall consist of five judges, until their number shall be increased, as herein provided. The present judge of the recorder's court of the city of Chicago, and the present judge of the circuit court of Cook county, shall be two of said judges, and shall remain in office for the terms for which they were respectively elected, and until their successors shall be elected and qualified. The superior court of Chicago shall be continued, and called the superior court of Cook county. The general assembly may increase the number of said judges, by adding one to either of said courts for every additional 50,000 inhabitants in said county over and above a population of 400,000. The terms of office of the judges of said courts hereafter elected shall be six years.

§ 24. The judge having the shortest unexpired term shall be chief justice of the court of which he is judge. In case there are two or more whose terms expire at the same time, it may be determined by lot which shall be chief justice. Any judge of either of said courts shall have all the powers of a circuit judge, and may hold the court of which he is a member. Each of them may hold a different branch thereof at the same time.

§ 25. The judges of the superior and circuit courts, and the State's attorney, in said county, shall receive the same salaries, payable out of the State treasury, as is or may be paid from said treasury to the circuit judges and the State's attorneys of the State, and such further compensation, to be paid by the said county of Cook, as is or may be provided by law ; such compensation shall not be changed during their continuance in office.

§ 26. The recorder's court of the city of Chicago shall be continued, and shall be called the "criminal court of Cook county." It shall have the jurisdiction of a circuit court, in all cases of criminal and *quasi* criminal nature, arising in the county of Cook, or that may be brought before said court pursuant to law; and all recognizances and appeals taken in said county, in criminal and *quasi* criminal cases, shall be returnable and taken to said court. It shall have no jurisdiction in civil cases, except those on behalf of the people, and incident to such criminal or *quasi* criminal matters, and to dispose of unfinished business. The terms of said criminal court of Cook county shall be held by one or more of the judges of the circuit or superior court of Cook county, as nearly as may be in alternation, as may be determined by said judges, or provided by law. Said judges shall be *ex-officio* judges of said court.

§ 27. The present clerk of the recorder's court of the city of Chicago shall be the clerk of the criminal court of Cook county during the term for which he was elected. The present clerks of the superior courts of Chicago, and the present clerk of the circuit court of Cook county, shall continue in office during the terms for which they were respectively elected; and thereafter there shall be but one clerk of the superior court, to be elected by the qualified electors of said county, who shall hold his office for the term of four years, and until his successor is elected and qualified.

§ 28. All justices of the peace in the city of Chicago shall be appointed by the governor, by and with the advice and consent of the senate, (but only upon the recommendation of a majority of the judges of the circuit, superior and county courts,) and for such districts as are now or shall hereafter be provided by law. They shall hold their offices for four years, and until their successors have been commissioned and qualified, but they may be removed by summary proceedings in the circuit or superior courts, for extortion or other malfeasance. Existing justices of the peace and police magistrates may hold their offices until the expiration of their respective terms.

GENERAL PROVISIONS.

§ 29. All judicial officers shall be commissioned by the governor. All laws relating to courts shall be general, and of uniform operation; and the organization, jurisdiction, powers, proceedings and practice of all courts, of the same class or grade, as far as regulated by law, and the force and effect of the process, judgments and decrees of such courts, severally, shall be uniform.

§ 30. The general assembly may, for cause entered on the journals, upon due notice and opportunity of defense, remove from office any judge, upon concurrence of three fourths of all the members elected of each house. All other officers in this article mentioned shall be removed from office, on prosecution and final conviction, for misdemeanor in office.

§ 31. All judges of courts of record, inferior to the supreme court, shall, on or before the first day of June of each year, report in writing to the judges of the supreme court, such defects and omissions in the laws as their experience may suggest ; and the judges of the supreme court shall, on or before the first day of January of each year, report in writing to the governor such defects and omissions in the constitution and laws as they may find to exist, together with appropriate forms of bills to cure such defects and omissions in the laws. And the judges of the several circuit courts shall report to the next general assembly the number of days they have held court in the several counties composing their respective circuits the preceding two years.

§ 32. All officers provided for in this article shall hold their offices until their successors shall be qualified, and they shall, respectively, reside in the division, circuit, county or district for which they may be elected or appointed. The terms of office of all such officers, where not otherwise prescribed in this article, shall be four years. All officers, where not otherwise provided for in this article, shall perform such duties and receive such compensation as is or may be provided by law. Vacancies in such elective offices shall be filled by election ; but where the unexpired term does not exceed one year, the vacancy shall be filled by appointment, as follows: Of judges, by the governor: of clerks of courts, by the court to which the office appertains, or by the judge or judges thereof; and of all such other offices, by the board of supervisors or board of county commissioners in the county where the vacancy occurs.

§ 33. All process shall run: *In the name of the People of the State of Illinois;* and all prosecutions shall be carried on: *In the name and by the authority of the People of the State of Illinois;* and conclude : *Against the peace and dignity of the same.* " Population," wherever used in this article, shall be determined by the next preceding census of this State, or of the United States.

ARTICLE VII.—SUFFRAGE.

§ 1. Every person having resided in this State one year, in the county ninety days, and in the election district thirty days next preceding any election therein, who was an elector in this State on the first day of April, in the year of our Lord 1848, or obtained a certificate of naturalization before any court of record in this State prior to the first day of January, in the year of our Lord 1870, or who shall be male citizen of the United States, above the age of twenty-one years, shall be entitled to vote at such election.

§ 2. All votes shall be by ballot.

§ 3. Electors shall, in all cases except treason, felony, or breach of the peace, be privileged from arrest during their attendance at elections, and in going to and returning from the same. And no elector shall be obliged to do military duty on the days of election, except in time of war or public danger.

§ 4. No elector shall be deemed to have lost his residence in this

State by reason of his absence on business of the United States, or in the military or naval service of the United States.

§ 5. No soldier, seaman or marine in the army or navy of the United States shall be deemed a resident of this State in consequence of being stationed therein.

§ 6. No person shall be elected or appointed to any office in this State, civil or military, who is not a citizen of the United States, and who shall not have resided in this State one year next preceding the election or appointment.

§ 7. The general assembly shall pass laws excluding from the right of suffrage persons convicted of infamous crimes.

ARTICLE VIII.—EDUCATION.

§ 1. The general assembly shall provide a thorough and efficient system of free schools, whereby all children of this State may receive a good common-school education.

§ 2. All lands, moneys, or other property, donated, granted, or received, for school, college, seminary or university purposes, and the proceeds thereof, shall be faithfully applied to the objects for which such grants were made.

§ 3. Neither the general assembly, nor any county, city, town, township, school district, or other public corporation, shall ever make any appropriation or pay from any public fund, whatever, anything in aid of any church or sectarian purpose, or to help support or sustain any school, academy, seminary, college, university, or other literary or scientific institution, controlled by any church or sectarian denomination whatever ; nor shall any grant or donation of land, money, or other personal property ever be made by the State or any such public corporation, to any church, or for any sectarian purposes.

§ 4. No teacher, State, county, township, or district school officer shall be interested in the sale, proceeds or profits of any book, apparatus or furniture, used or to be used, in any school in this State, with which such officer or teacher may be connected, under such penalties as may be provided by the general assembly.

§ 5. There may be a county superintendent of schools in each county, whose qualifications, powers, duties, compensation. and time and manner of election, and term of office, shall be prescribed by law.

ARTICLE IX.—REVENUE.

§ 1. The general assembly shall provide such revenue as may be needful by levying a tax, by valuation, so that every person and corporation shall pay a tax in proportion to the value of his, her or its property—such value to be ascertained by some person or persons, to be elected or appointed in such manner as the general assembly shall direct, and not otherwise ; but the general assembly shall have power to tax peddlers, auctioneers, brokers, hawkers, merchants, commission merchants, showmen, jugglers, inn-keepers, grocery keepers, liquor dealers, toll bridges, ferries, insurance, telegraph and express interests or business, venders of patents, and persons or corporations owning or using franchises and privileges, in such manner as it shall from time to time direct by general law, uniform as to the class upon which it operates.

§ 2. The specification of the objects and subjects of taxation shall not deprive the general assembly of the power to require other subjects or objects to be taxed in such manner as may be consistent with the principles of taxation fixed in this constitution.

§ 3. The property of the State, counties, and other municipal corporations, both real and personal, and such other property as may be used exclusively for agricultural and horticultural societies, for school, religious, cemetery and charitable purposes, may be exempted from taxation ; but such exemption shall be only by general law. In the assessment of real estate incumbered by public easement, any depreciation occasioned by such easement may be deducted in the valuation of such property.

§ 4. The general assembly shall provide, in all cases where it may be necessary to sell real estate for the non-payment of taxes or special assessments for State, county, municipal or other purposes, that a return of such unpaid taxes or assessments shall be made to some general officer of the county having authority to receive State and county taxes ; and there shall be no sale of said property for any of said taxes or assessments but by said officer, upon the order or judgment of some court of record.

§ 5. The right of redemption from all sales of real estate for the non payment of taxes or special assessments of any character whatever, shall exist in favor of owners and persons interested in such real estate for a period of not less than two years from such sales thereof. And the general assembly shall provide by law for reasonable notice to be given to the owners or parties interested, by publication or otherwise, of the fact of the sale of the property for such taxes or assessments, and when the time of redemption shall expire : *Provided*, that occupants shall in all cases be served with personal notice before the time of redemption expires.

§ 6. The general assembly shall have no power to release or discharge any county, city, or township, town or district whatever, or the inhabitants thereof, or the property therein, from their or its proportionate share of taxes to be levied for State purposes, nor shall commutation for such taxes be authorized in any form whatsoever.

§ 7. All taxes levied for State purposes shall be paid into the State treasury.

§ 8. County authorities shall never assess taxes, the aggregate of which shall exceed 75 cents per $100 valuation, except for the payment of indebtedness existing at the adoption of this constitution, unless authorized by a vote of the people of the county.

§ 9. The general assembly may vest the corporate authorities of cities, towns and villages with power to make local improvements by special assessment or by special taxation of contiguous property, or otherwise. For all other corporate purposes, all municipal corporations may be vested with authority to assess and collect taxes, but such taxes shall be uniform in respect to persons and property within the jurisdiction of the body imposing the same.

§ 10. The general assembly shall not impose taxes upon municipal corporations, or the inhabitants or property thereof, for corporate purposes, but shall require that all the taxable property within the limits of municipal corporations shall be taxed for the payment of debts contracted under authority of law, such taxes to be uniform in respect to persons and property within the jurisdiction of the body imposing the same. Private property shall not be liable to be taken or sold for the payment of the corporate debts of a municipal corporation.

§ 11. No person who is in default, as collector or custodian of money or property belonging to a municipal corporation shall be eligible to any office in or under such corporation. The fees, salary or compensation of no municipal officer who is elected or appointed for a definite term of office shall be increased or diminished during such term.

§ 12. No county, city, township, school district, or other municipal corporation shall be allowed to become indebted in any manner or for any purpose to an amount, including existing indebtedness, in the aggregate exceeding five per centum on the value of the taxable property therein, to be ascertained by the last assessment for State and county taxes previous to the incurring of such indebtedness. Any county, city, school district, or other municipal corporation, incurring any indebtedness as aforesaid, shall, before, or at the time of doing so, provide for the collection of a direct annual tax sufficient to pay the interest on such debt as it falls due, and also to pay and discharge the principal thereof within twenty years from the time of contracting the same. This section shall not be construed to prevent any county, city, township, school district, or other municipal corporation from issuing their bonds in compliance with any vote of the people which may have been had prior to the adoption of this constitution in pursuance of any law providing therefor.

ARTICLE X.—COUNTIES.

§ 1. No new county shall be formed or established by the general assembly which will reduce the county or counties, or either of them, from which it shall be taken, to less contents than 400 square miles ; nor shall any county be formed of less contents : nor shall any line thereof pass within less than ten miles of any county seat of the county or counties proposed to be divided.

§ 2. No county shall be divided, or have any part stricken therefrom, without submitting the question to a vote of the people of the county, nor unless a majority of all the legal voters of the county voting on the question shall vote for the same.

§ 3. There shall be no territory stricken from any county, unless a majority of the voters living in such territory shall petition for such division; and no territory shall be added to any county without the consent of the majority of the voters of the county to which it is proposed to be added. But the portion so stricken off and added to another county, or formed in whole or in part into a new county, shall be holden for, and obliged to pay, its proportion of the indebtedness of the county from which it has been taken.

COUNTY SEATS.

§ 4. No county seat shall be removed until the point to which it is proposed to be removed shall be fixed in pursuance of law, and three-fifths of the voters of the county, to be ascertained in such manner as shall be provided by general law, shall have voted in favor of its removal to such point; and no person shall vote on such question who has not resided in the county six months, and in the election precinct ninety days next preceding such election. The question of the removal of a county seat shall not be oftener submitted than once in ten years to a vote of the people. But when an attempt is made to remove a county seat to a point nearer to the centre of a county, then a majority vote only shall be necessary.

COUNTY GOVERNMENT.

§ 5. The general assembly shall provide, by general law, for township organization, under which any county may organize whenever a majority of the legal voters of such county, voting at any general election, shall so determine, and whenever any county shall adopt township organization, so much of this constitution as provides for the management of the fiscal concerns of the said county by the board of county commissioners, may be dispensed with, and the affairs of said county may be transacted in such a manner as the general assembly may provide. And in any county that shall have adopted a township organization the question of continuing the same may be submitted to a vote of the electors of such county at a general election, in the manner that now is or may be provided by law; and if a majority of all the votes cast upon that question shall be against township organization, then such organization shall cease in said county; and all laws in force in relation to counties not having township organization, shall immediately take effect and be in force in such county. No two townships shall have the same name, and the day of holding the annual township meeting shall be uniform throughout the State.

§ 6. At the first election of county judges under this constitution there shall be elected in each of the counties of this State, not under township organization, three officers, who shall be styled "The Board of County Commissioners," who shall hold sessions for the transaction of county business as shall be provided by law. One of said commissioners shall hold his office for one year, one for two years, and one for three years, to be determined by lot; and every year thereafter one such officer shall be elected in each of said counties for the term of three years.

§ 7. The county affairs of Cook county shall be managed by a board of commissioners of fifteen persons, ten of whom shall be elected from the city of Chicago and five from towns outside of said city, in such manner as may be provided by law.

COUNTY OFFICERS AND THEIR COMPENSATION.

* § 8. In each county there shall be elected the following county officers, at the general election to be held on the Tuesday after the first Monday in November A.D. 1882: A county judge, county clerk, sheriff and treasurer ; and at the election to be held on the Tuesday after the first Monday in November A.D 1884. a coroner and clerk of the circuit court (who may be ex officio recorder of deeds, except in counties having 60,000 or more inhabitants, in which counties a recorder of deeds shall be elected at the general election in 1884). Each

---

* NOTE.—Sec. 8 is an amendment adopted Nov. 2, 1880.

of said officers shall enter upon the duties of his office respectively on the first Monday of December after his election, and they shall hold their respective offices for the term of four years, and until their successors are elected and qualified; *Provided,* That no person having once been elected to the office of sheriff or treasurer, shall be eligible to re-election to said office for four years after the expiration of the term for which he shall have been elected.

§ 9. The clerks of all the courts of record, the treasurer, sheriff, coroner and recorder of deeds of Cook county, shall receive as their only compensation for their services salaries to be fixed by law, which shall in no case be as much as the lawful compensation of a judge of the circuit court of said county, and shall be paid, respectively, only out of the fees of the office actually collected. All fees, perquisites, and emoluments (above the amount of said salaries) shall be paid into the county treasury. The number of deputies and assistants of such officers shall be determined by rule of the circuit court, to be entered of record, and their compensation shall be determined by the county board.

§ 10. The county board, except as provided in § 9 of this article, shall fix the compensation of all county officers, with the amount of their necessary clerk hire, stationery, fuel, and other expenses, and in all cases where fees are provided for, said compensation shall be paid only out of, and shall in no instance exceed, the fees actually collected; they shall not allow either of them more per annum than $1,500 in counties not exceeding 20,000 inhabitants; $2,000 in counties containing 20,000 and not exceeding 30,000 inhabitants; $2,500 in counties containing 30,000 and not exceeding 50,000 inhabitants; $3,000 in counties containing 50,000 and not exceeding 70,000 inhabitants; $3,500 in counties containing 70,000 and not exceeding 100,000 inhabitants; and $4,000 in counties containing over 100,000 and not exceeding 250,000 inhabitants; and not more than $1,000 additional compensation for each additional 100,000 inhabitants: *Provided,* that the compensation of no officer shall be increased or diminished during his term of office. All fees or allowances by them received, in excess of their said compensation, shall be paid into the county treasury.

§ 11. The fees of township officers, and of each class of county officers, shall be uniform in the class of counties to which they respectively belong. The compensation herein provided for shall apply only to officers hereafter elected, but all fees established by special laws shall cease at the adoption of this constitution, and such officers shall receive only such fees as are provided by general law.

§ 12. All laws fixing the fees of State, county and township officers, shall terminate with the terms, respectively, of those who may be in office at the meeting of the first general assembly after the adoption of this constitution ; and the general assembly shall, by general law, uniform in its operation, provide for and regulate the fees of said officers and their successors, so as to reduce the same to a reasonable compensation for services actually rendered. But the general assembly may, by general law, classify the counties by population into not more than three classes, and regulate the fees according to class. This article shall not be construed as depriving the general assembly of the power to reduce the fees of existing officers.

§ 13. Every person who is elected or appointed to any office in this State, who shall be paid in whole or in part by fees, shall be required by law to make a semi-annual report, under oath, to some officer to be designated by law, of all his fees and emoluments.

ARTICLE XI.—CORPORATIONS.

§ 1. No corporation shall be created by special laws, or its charter extended, changed or amended, except those for charitable, educational, penal, or reformatory purposes, which are to be and remain under the patronage and control of the State, but the general assembly shall provide, by general laws, for the organization of all corporations hereafter to be created.

§ 2. All existing charters or grants of special or exclusive privileges, under which organization shall not have taken place, or which shall not have been in operation within ten days from the time this constitution takes effect, shall thereafter have no validity or effect whatever.

§ 3. The general assembly shall provide, by law, that in all elections for directors or managers of incorporated companies, every stockholder shall have the right to vote, in person or by proxy, for the number of shares of stock owned by him, for as many persons as there are directors or managers to be elected. or to cumulate said shares, and give one candidate as many votes as the number of directors multiplied by the number of his shares of stock shall equal, or to distribute them on the same principle among as many candidates as he shall think fit; and such directors or managers shall not be elected in any other manner.

§ 4. No law shall be passed by the general assembly granting the right to construct and operate a street railroad within any city, town, or incorporated village, without requiring the consent of the local authorities having the control of the street or highway proposed to be occupied by such street railroad.

BANKS.

§ 5. No State bank shall hereafter be created, nor shall the State own or be liable for any stock in any corporation or joint stock company or association for banking purposes, now created, or to be hereafter created. No act of the general assembly authorizing or creating corporations or associations, with banking powers, whether of issue, deposit or discount, nor amendments thereto, shall go into effect, or in any manner be in force, unless the same shall be submitted to a vote of the people at the general election next succeeding the passage of the same, and be approved by a majority of all the votes cast at such election for or against such law.

§ 6. Every stockholder in a banking corporation or institution shall be individually responsible and liable to its creditors, over and above the amount of stock by him or her held, to an amount equal to his or her respective shares so held, for all its liabilities accruing while he or she remains such stockholder.

§ 7. The suspension of specie payments by banking institutions, on their circulation, created by the laws of this State, shall never be permitted or sanctioned. Every banking association now, or which may hereafter be, organized under the laws of this State, shall make and publish a full and accurate quarterly statement of its affairs (which shall be certified to, under oath, by one or more of its officers) as may be provided by law.

§ 8. If a general banking law shall be enacted, it shall provide for the registry and countersigning by an officer of state, of all bills or paper credit, designed to circulate as moneys, and require security, to the full amount thereof, to be deposited with the State treasurer, in United States or Illinois State stocks, to be rated at ten per cent. below their par value; and in case of a depreciation of said stocks to the amount of ten per cent. below par, the bank or banks owning said stocks shall be required to make up said deficiency by depositing additional stocks. And said law shall also provide for the recording of the names of all stockholders in such corporations, the amount of stock held by each, the time of any transfer thereof, and to whom such transfer is made.

RAILROADS.

§ 9. Every railroad corporation organized or doing business in this State, under the laws or authority thereof shall have and maintain a public office or place in this State for the transaction of its business, where transfers of stock shall be made, and in which shall be kept, for public inspection, books, in which shall be recorded the amount of capital stock subscribed, and by whom; the names of the owners of its stock, and the amounts owned by them, respectively; the amount of stock paid in, and by whom; the transfers of said stock; the amount of its assets and liabilities, and the names and place of residence of its officers. The directors of every railroad corporation shall, annually, make a report, under oath, to the auditor, of public accounts, or some officer to be designated by law, of all their acts and doings, which report shall include such matters relating to railroads as may be prescribed by law. And the general assembly shall pass laws enforcing, by suitable penalties, the provisions of this section.

§ 10. The rolling stock, and all other movable property belonging to any railroad company or corporation in this State, shall be considered personal property, and shall be liable to execution and sale in the same manner as the personal property of individuals, and the general assembly shall pass no law exempting any such property from execution and sale.

§ 11. No railroad corporation shall consolidate its stock, property or franchises with any other railroad corporation owning a parallel or competing line; and in no case shall any consolidation take place except upon public notice given, of at least sixty days, to all stockholders, in such manner as may be provided by law. A majority of the directors of any railroad corporation, now incorporated or hereafter to be incorporated by the laws of this State, shall be citizens and residents of this State.

§ 12. Railways heretofore constructed, or that may hereafter be constructed in this State, are hereby declared public highways, and shall be free to all persons for the transportation of their persons and property thereon, under such regulations as may be prescribed by law. And the general assembly shall, from time to time, pass laws establishing reasonable maximum rates of charges for the transportation of passengers and freight on the different railroads in this State.

§ 13. No railroad corporation shall issue any stock or bonds, except for money, labor or property actually received, and applied to the purposes for which such corporation was created; and all stock dividends, and other fictitious increase of the capital stock or indebtedness of any such corporation, shall be void. The capital stock of no railroad corporation shall be increased for any purpose, except upon giving sixty days' public notice, in such manner as may be provided by law.

§ 14. The exercise of the power, and the right of eminent domain shall never be so construed or abridged as to prevent the taking by the general assembly, of the property and franchises of incorporated companies already organized, and subjecting them to the public necessity the same as of individuals. The right of trial by jury shall be held inviolate in all trials of claims for compensation, when, in the exercise of the said right of eminent domain, any incorporated company shall be interested either for or against the exercise of said right.

§ 15. The general assembly shall pass laws to correct abuses and prevent unjust discrimination and extortion in the rates of freight and passenger tariffs on the different railroads in this State, and enforce such laws, by adequate penalties, to the extent, if necessary for that purpose, of forfeiture of their property and franchises.

ARTICLE XII.—MILITIA.

§ 1. The militia of the State of Illinois shall consist of all able-bodied male persons, resident in the State, between the ages of eighteen and forty-five, except such persons as now are, or hereafter may be, exempted by the laws of the United States, or of this S'ate.

§ 2. The general assembly, in providing for the organization, equipment and discipline of the militia, shall conform as nearly as practicable to the regulations for the government of the armies of the United States.

§ 3. All militia officers shall be commissioned by the governor, and may hold their commissions for such time as the general assembly may provide.

§ 4. The militia shall, in all cases, except treason, felony or breach of the peace, be privileged from arrest during their attendance at musters and elections and in g ing to and returning from the same.

§ 5. The military records, banners and relics of the State shall be preserved as an enduring memorial of the patriotism and valor of Illinois, and it shall be the duty of the general assembly to provide by law for the safe keeping of the same.

§ 6. No person having conscientious scruples against bearing arms shall be compelled to do military duty in time of peace : *Provided*, such person shall pay an equivalent for such exemption.

ARTICLE XIII.—WAREHOUSES.

§ 1. All elevators or storehouses where grain or other property is stored for compensation, whether the property stored be kept separate or not, are declared to be public warehouses.

§ 2. The owner, lessee or manager of each and every public warehouse situated in any town or city of not less than 100,000 inhabitants, shall make weekly statements, under oath, before some officer to be designated by law, and keep the same posted in some conspicuous place in the office of such warehouse, and shall also file a copy for public examination in such place as shall be designated by law, which statement shall correctly set forth the am unt and grade of each and every kind of grain in such warehouse, together with such other property as may be stored therein, and what warehouse receipts have been issued, and are, at the time of making such statement, outstanding therefor; and shall, on the copy posted in the warehouse, note daily such changes as may be made in the quantity and grade of grain in such warehouse ; and the different grades of grain shipped in separate lots shall not be mixed with inferior or superior grades without the consent of the owner or consignee thereof.

§ 3. The owners of property stored in any warehouse, or holder of a receipt for same, shall always be at liberty to examine such property stored, and all the books and records of the warehouse in regard to such property.

§ 4. All railroad companies and other common carriers on railroads shall weigh or measure grain at points where it is shipped, and receipt for the full amount, and shall be responsible for the delivery of such amount to the owner or consignee thereof at the place of destination.

§ 5. All railroad companies receiving and transporting grain, in bulk or otherwise, shall deliver the same to any consignee thereof, or any elevator or public warehouse to which it may be consigned, provided such consignee, or the elevator or public warehouse, can be reached by any track owned, leased or used, or which can be used, by such railroad companies ; and all railroad companies shall permit connections to be made with their track, so that any such consignee, and any public warehouse, coal bank or coal yard, may be reached by the cars on said railroad.

§ 6 It shall be the duty of the general assembly to pass all necessary laws to prevent the issue of false and fraudulent warehouse receipts, and to give full effect to this article of the constitution, which shall be liberally construed so as to protect producers and shippers. And the enumeration of the remedies herein named shall not be construed to deny to the general assembly the power to prescribe by law such other and further remedies as may be found expedient, or to deprive any person of existing common law remedies.

§ 7. The general assembly shall pass laws for the inspection of grain, for the protection of producers, shippers and receivers of grain and produce.

ARTICLE XIV.—AMENDMENTS TO THE CONSTITUTION.

§ 1. Whenever two-thirds of the members of each house of the general assembly shall, by a vote entered upon the journal thereof, concur that a convention is necessary to revise, alter or amend the constitution, the question shall be submitted to the electors at the next general election. If a majority voting at the election vote for a convention, the general assembly shall, at the next session, provide for a convention, to consist of double the number of members of the senate, to be elected in the same manner, at the same places, and in the same districts. The general assembly shall, in the act calling the convention, designate the day, hour, and place of its meeting, fix the pay of its members and officers, and provide for the payment of the same, together with expenses necessarily incurred by the convention in the performance of its duties. Before proceeding, the members shall take an oath to support the constitution of the United States, and of the State of Illinois, and to faithfully discharge their duties as members of the convention. The qualification of members shall be the same as that of members of the senate, and vacancies occurring shall be filled in the manner provided for filling vacancies in the general assembly. Said convention shall meet within three months after such election, and prepare such revision, alteration or amendments of the constitution as shall be deemed necessary, which shall be submitted to the electors for their ratification or rejection, at an election appointed by the convention for that purpose, not less than two nor more than six months after the adjournment thereof ; and unless so submitted and approved by a majority of the electors voting at the election, no such revision, alterations or amendments shall take effect.

§ 2. Amendments to this constitution may be proposed in either house of the general assembly, and if the same shall be voted for by two thirds of all the members elected to each of the two houses, such proposed amendments, together with the yeas and nays of each house thereon, shall be entered in full on their respective journals, and said amendments shall be submitted to the electors of this State for adoption or rejection, at the next election of members of the general assembly, in such manner as may be prescribed by law. The proposed amendments shall be published in full at least three months preceding the election, and if a majority of the electors voting at said election shall vote for the proposed amendments, they shall become a part of this constitution. But the general assembly shall have no power to propose amendments to more than one article of this constitution at the same session, nor to the same article oftener than once in four years.

SEPARATE SECTIONS.

No contract, obligation, or liability whatever, of the Illinois Central Railroad Company, to pay any money into the State treasury, nor any lien of the State upon, or right to tax property of said company, in accordance with the provisions of the charter of said company, approved February 10, in the year of our Lord 1851, shall ever be released, suspended, modified, altered, remitted, or in any manner diminished or impaired by legislative or other authority; and all moneys derived from said company, after the payment of the State debt, shall be appropriated and set apart for the payment of the ordinary expenses of the State government, and for no other purposes whatever.

MUNICIPAL SUBSCRIPTIONS TO RAILROADS OR PRIVATE CORPORATIONS.

No county, city, town, township, or other municipality, shall ever become subscriber to the capital stock of any railroad or private corporation, or make donation to or loan its credit in aid of such corporation : *Provided, however,* that the adoption of this article shall not be construed as affecting the right of any such municipality to make such subscriptions where the same have been authorized, under existing laws, by a vote of the people of such municipalities prior to such adoption.

CANAL.

The Illinois and Michigan Canal shall never be sold or leased until the specific proposition for the sale or lease thereof shall first have been submitted to a vote of the people of the State at a general election, and have been approved by a majority of all the votes polled at such election. The general assembly shall never loan the credit of the State, or make appropriations from the treasury thereof, in aid of railroads or canals : *Provided,* that any surplus earnings of any canal may be appropriated for its enlargement or extension.

SCHEDULE.

That no inconvenience may arise from the alterations and amendments made in the constitution of this State, and to carry the same into complete effect, it is hereby ordained and declared :

§ 1. That all laws in force at the adoption of this constitution not inconsistent therewith, and all rights, actions, prosecutions, claims, and contracts of this State, individuals, or bodies corporate, shall continue to be as valid as if this constitution had not been adopted.

§ 2. That all fines, taxes, penalties and forfeitures, due and owing to the State of Illinois under the present constitution and laws, shall inure to the use of the people of the State of Illinois under this constitution.

§ 3. Recognizances, bonds, obligation, and all other instruments entered into or executed before the adoption of this constitution, to the people of the State of Illinois, to any State or county officer or public body, shall remain binding and valid ; and rights and liabilities upon the same shall continue, and all crimes and misdemeanors shall be tried and punished as though no change had been made in the constitution of this State.

§ 4. County courts for the transaction of county business in counties not having adopted township organization, shall continue in existence and exercise their present jurisdiction until the board of county commissioners provided in this constitution is organized in pursuance of an act of the general assembly ; and the county courts in all other counties shall have the same power and jurisdiction they now possess until otherwise provided by general law.

§ 5. All existing courts which are not in this constitution specifically enumerated, shall continue in existence and exercise their present jurisdiction until otherwise provided by law.

§ 6. All persons now filling any office or appointment shall continue in the exercise of the duties thereof according to their respective commissions or appointments, unless by this constitution it is otherwise directed.

§ 7. On the day this constitution is submitted to the people for ratification, an election shall be held for judges of the supreme court, in the second, third, sixth and seventh judicial election districts, designated in this constitution, and for the election of three judges of the circuit court in the county of Cook, as provided for in the article of this constitution relating to the judiciary ; at which election every person entitled to vote, according to the terms of this constitution, shall be allowed to vote, and the election shall be otherwise conducted, returns made and certificates issued, in accordance with existing laws, except that no registry shall be required at said election ; *Provided*, that at said election in the county of Cook no elector shall vote for more than two candidates for circuit judge. If, upon canvassing the votes for and against the adoption of this constitution, it shall appear that there has been polled a greater number against than for it, then no certificates of election shall be issued for any of said supreme or circuit judges.

§ S. This constitution shall be submitted to the people of the State of Illinois for adoption or rejection, at an election to be held on the first Saturday in July, A. D 1870, and there shall be separately submitted at the same time, for adoption or rejection :

Sections nine, ten, eleven, twelve, thirteen, fourteen and fifteen, relating to railroads, in the article entitled corporations ;

The article entitled counties ;

The article entitled warehouses ;

The question of requiring three-fifths vote to remove a county seat :

The section relating to the Illinois Central railroad ;

The section relating to minority representation;

The section relating to municipal subscriptions to railroads or private corporations, and

The section relating to the canal.

Every person entitled to vote under the provisions of this constitution, as defined in the article in relation to " suffrage," shall be entitled to vote for the adoption or rejection of this constitution, and for or against the articles, sections and questions aforesaid, separately submitted ; and the said qualified electors shall vote at the usual places of voting. unless otherwise provided. and the said elections shall be conducted, and the returns thereof made, according to the laws now in force regulating general elections, except that no registry shall be required at said election ; *Provided, however*, that the polls shall be kept open for the reception of ballots until sunset of said day of election.

§ 9. The Secretary of State shall, at least twenty days before said election, cause to be delivered to the county clerk of each county, blank poll-books, tally-lists and forms of return and twice the number of properly prepared printed ballots for the said election that there are voters in such county, the expense whereof shall be audited and paid as other public printing ordered by the Secretary of State is, by law, required to be audited and paid ; and the several county clerks shall, at least five days before said election, cause to be distributed to the board of election, in each election district, in their respective counties, said blank poll-books, tally lists, forms of return, and tickets.

§ 10. At the said election the ballots shall be in the following form :

NEW CONSTITUTION TICKET.

For all the propositions on this ticket which are not canceled with ink or pencil ; and against all propositions which are so canceled.

For the new constitution.

For the sections relating to railroads in the article entitled corporations.

For the article entitled counties.

For the article entitled warehouses.

For a three-fifths vote to remove county seats.

For the sections relating to the Illinois Central railroad.

For the section relating to minority representation.

For the section relating to municipal subscriptions to railroads or private corporations.

For the section relating to the canal.

Each of said tickets shall be counted as a vote cast for each proposition thereon not canceled with ink or pencil, and against each proposition so canceled, and returns thereof shall be made accordingly by the judges of election.

§ 11. The returns of the whole vote cast, and of the votes for the adoption or rejection of this Constitution, and for or against the articles and sections respectively submitted, shall be made by the several county clerks, as is now provided by law, to the Secretary of State, within twenty days after the election ; and the returns of the said votes shall, within five days thereafter, be examined and canvassed by the Auditor, Treasurer and Secretary of State, or any two of them, in the presence of the Governor, and proclamation shall be made by the Governor, forthwith, of the result of the canvass.

§ 12. If it shall appear that a majority of the votes polled are "for the new Constitution," then so much of this Constitution as was not separately submitted to be voted on by articles and sections shall be the supreme law of the State of Illinois, on and after Monday, the 8th day of August, A. D. 1870 ; but if it shall appear that a majority of the votes polled were "against the new Constitution," then so much thereof as was not separately submitted to be voted on by articles and sections shall be null and void. If it shall appear that a majority of the votes polled are "for the sections relating to railroads in the article entitled 'corporations,'" sections nine, ten, eleven, twelve, thirteen, fourteen and fifteen, relating to railroads in the said article, shall be a part of the Constitution of this State, but if a majority of said votes are against such sections, they shall be null and void If a majority of the votes polled are "for the article entitled "counties," such article shall be a part of the Constitution of this State, and shall be substituted for article seven in the present Constitution, entitled "counties;" but if a majority of said votes are against such article, the same shall be null and void. If a majority of votes polled are for the article entitled "warehouses," such article shall be a part of the Constitution of this State ; but if a majority of the votes are against said article, the same shall be null and void. If a majority of the votes polled are for either of the sections separately submitted relating respectively to the "Illinois Central railroad," "minority representation," "municipal subscriptions to railroads or private corporations," and the "canal," then such of said sections as shall receive such majority shall be a part of the Constitution of this State ; but each of said sections so separately submitted, against which, respectively, there shall be a majority of the votes polled, shall be null and void ; *Provided*, that the section relating to "minority representation," shall not be declared adopted unless the portion of the Constitution not separately submitted to be voted on by articles and sections shall be adopted ; and in case said section relating to "minority representation " shall become a part of the Constitution it shall be substituted for sections seven and eight of the legislative articles. If a majority of the votes cast at such election shall be for a three-fifths vote to remove a county seat, then the words "a majority" shall be stricken out of section four of the article on counties, and the words "three-fifths" shall be inserted in lieu thereof ; and the following words shall be added to said section, to-wit : "But when an attempt is made to remove a county seat to a point nearer to the centre of a county, then a majority vote shall only be necessary." If the foregoing proposition shall not receive a majority of the votes as aforesaid, then the same shall have no effect whatever.

§ 13. Immediately after the adoption of this Constitution, the Governor and Secretary of State shall proceed to ascertain and fix the apportionment of the State for members of the first house of Representatives under this Constitution. The apportionment shall be based upon the federal census of the year A. D. 1870. of the State of Illinois, and shall be made strictly in accordance with the rules and principles announced in the article on the legislative department of this Constitution : *Provided*, that in case the federal census aforesaid cannot be ascertained prior to Friday, the 23d day of September, A. D. 1870, then the said apportionment shall be based upon the State census of the year A. D. 1865, in accordance with the rules and principles aforesaid. The Governor shall, on or before Wednesday, the 28th day of September, A. D. 1870, make official announcement of the said apportionment, under the great seal of the State, and one hundred copies thereof, duly certified, shall be forthwith transmitted by the Secretary of State to each county clerk for distribution.

§ 14. The districts shall be regularly numbered by the Secretary of State, commencing with Alexander County as No. 1, and proceeding thence northwardly through the State, and terminating with the county of Cook ; but no county shall be numbered as more than one district, except the county of Cook, which shall constitute three districts, each embracing the territory contained in the now existing representative districts of said county. And on the Tuesday after the first Monday in November, A. D. 1870, the members of the first house of representatives under this Constitution shall be elected according to the apportionment fixed and announced as aforesaid, and shall hold their offices for two years, and until their successors shall be elected and qualified.

§ 15. The senate, at its first session under this Constitution, shall consist of fifty members, to be chosen as follows . At the general election held on the first Tuesday after the first Monday of November, A. D. 1870, two senators shall be elected in districts where term of senators expire on the first Monday of January, A. D. 1871, or where there shall be a vacancy, and in the remaining districts one senator shall be elected. Senators so elected shall hold their office for two years.

§ 16. The general assembly, at its first session held after the adoption of this Constitution, shall proceed to apportion the State for members of the senate and house of representatives, in accordance with the provisions of the article on the legislative department.

§ 17. When this Constitution shall be ratified by the people, the Governor shall forthwith, after having ascertained the fact, issue writs of election to the sheriffs of the several counties of this State, or in case of vacancies, to the coroners, for the election of all the officers, the time of whose election is fixed by this Constitution or schedule, and it shall be the duties of said sheriffs or coroners to give such notice of the time and place of said election as is now prescribed by law.

§ 18. All laws of the State of Illinois, and all official writings, and the executive, legislative and judicial proceedings, shall be conducted, preserved and published in no other than the English language.

§ 19. The general assembly shall pass all laws necessary to carry into effect the provisions of this Constitution.

§ 20. The circuit clerks of the different counties having a population over sixty thousand, shall continue to be recorders (*ex-officio*) for their respective counties under this Constitution, until the expiration of their respective terms.

§ 21. The judges of all courts of record in Cook county shall, in lieu of any salary provided for in this Constitution, receive the compensation now provided by law until the adjournment of the first ssssion of the general assembly after the adoption of this Constitution.

§ 22. The present judge of the circuit court of Cook county sh»ll continue to hold the circuit court of Lake county until otherwise provided by law.

§ 23. When this Constitution shall be adopted, and take effect as the supreme law of the State of Illinois, the two-mill tax provided to be annually assessed and collected upon each dollar's worth of taxable property in addition to all other taxes, as set forth in article fifteen of the now existing Constitution, shall cease to be assessed after the year of our Lord one thousand eight hundred and seventy.

§ 24. Nothing contained in this Constitution shall be so construed as to deprive the general assembly of power to authorize the city of Quincy to create any indebtedness for railroad or municipal purposes, for which the people of said city shall have voted, and to which they shall have given, by such vote, their assent, prior to the thirteenth day of December, in the year of our Lord one thousand eight hundred and sixty-nine : *Provided*, that no such indebtedness so created shall in any part thereof be paid by the State, or from any State revenue, tax or fund, but the same shall be paid, if at all, by the said city of Quincy alone, and by taxes levied upon the taxable property thereof : *And provided further*, that the general assembly shall have no power in the premises that it could not exercise under the present Constitution of this State.

§ 25. In case this Constitution and the articles and sections submitted separately be adopted, the existing Constitution shall cease in all its provisions ; and in case this Constitution be adopted, and any one or more of the articles or sections submitted separately be defeated, the provisions of the existing Constitution (if any) on the same subject shall remain in force

§ 26. The provisions of this Constitution required to be executed prior to the adoption or rejection thereof shall take effect and be in force immediately.

Done in convention at the capitol, in the city of Springfield, on the thirteenth day of May, in the year of our Lord one thousand eight hundred and seventy, and of the independence of the United States of America the ninety-fourth.

THE FOLLOWING AMENDMENT TO SEC. 31, ART. 4, WAS ADOPTED IN 1878:

The General Assembly may pass laws permitting the owners of lands to construct drains, ditches and levees for agricultural, sanitary or mining purposes, across the lands of others, and provide for the organization of drainage districts, and vest the corporate authorities thereof with power to construct and maintain levees, drains and ditches, and to keep in repair all drains, ditches, and levees hereto-fore constructed under the laws of this State, by special assessments upon the property benefited thereby.

CONSTITUTION OF THE UNITED STATES.

We, the people of the United States, in order to form a more perfect Union, establish justice, insure domestic tranquility, provide for the common defence, promote the general welfare, and secure the blessings of liberty to ourselves and our posterity, do ordain and establish this Constitution for the United States of America. *Preamble.*

ARTICLE I.

SECTION I.

All legislative powers herein granted shall be vested in a Congress of the United States, which shall consist of a Senate and House of Representatives. *Congress.*

SECTION II.

The House of Representatives shall be composed of members chosen every second year by the people of the several States, and the electors in each State shall have the qualifications requisite for electors of the most numerous branch of the State legislature. *Representatives, how chosen.*

No person shall be a Representative who shall not have attained the age of twenty five years, and been seven years a citizen of the United States, and who shall not, when elected, be an inhabitant of that State in which he shall be chosen. *Qualifications of representatives.*

Representatives and direct taxes shall be apportioned among the several States which may be included within this Union, according to their respective numbers, which shall be determined by adding to the whole number of free persons, including those bound to service for a term of years, and excluding Indians not taxed, three-fifths of all other persons. The actual enumeration shall be made within three years after the first meeting of the Congress of the United States, and within every subsequent term of ten years, in such manner as they shall *Apportionment of representatives and direct taxes.* *Census every ten years.*

179

by law direct. The number of Representatives shall not exceed one for every thirty thousand, but each State shall have at least one representative; and until such enumeration shall be made, the State of *New Hampshire* shall be entitled to choose three, *Massachusetts,* eight, *Rhode Island and Providence Plantations* one, *Connecticut* five, *New York* six, *New Jersey* four, *Pennsylvania* eight, *Delaware* one, *Maryland* six, *Virginia* ten, *North Carolina* five, *South Carolina* five, and *Georgia* three.

Vacancies, how filled.

When vacancies happen in the representation from any State, the executive authority thereof shall issue writs of election to fill such vacancies.

Representatives choose officers and bring impeachments.

The House of Representatives shall choose their Speaker and other officers; and shall have the sole power of impeachment.

SECTION III.

Senate, how chosen.

The Senate of the United States shall be composed of two Senators from each State, chosen by the legislature thereof, for six years; and each Senator shall have one vote.

Senators classed.

Immediately after they shall be assembled in consequence of the first election, they shall be divided as equally as may be into three classes. The seats of the Senators of the first class shall be vacated at the expiration of the second year; of the second class, at the expiration of the fourth year, and of the third class, at the expiration of the sixth year, so that one-third may be chosen every second year; and if vacancies happen by resignation or otherwise, during the recess of the legislature of any State, the executive thereof may make temporary appointments until the next meeting of the legislature, which shall then fill such vacancies.

Vacancies, how filled.

Qualification of Senators.

No person shall be a Senator, who shall not have attained to the age of thirty years, and been nine years a citizen of the United States, and who shall not, when elected, be an inhabitant of that State for which he shall be chosen.

Vice President to preside.

The Vice President of the United States shall be President of the Senate, but shall have no vote, unless they be equally divided.

Officers of Senate.

The Senate shall choose their other officers, and also a President *pro tempore* in the absence of the Vice President, or when he shall exercise the office of President of the United States.

The Senate shall have the sole power to try all impeachments. When sitting for that purpose, they shall be on oath or affirmation. When the President of the United States is tried, the Chief Justice shall preside ; and *Trial of impeachments.* no person shall be convicted without the concurrence of two thirds of the members present.

Judgment in cases of impeachment shall not ex- *Judgment in impeachments.* tend further than to removal from office, and disqualification to hold and enjoy any office of honor, *Effect of.* trust or profit under the United States ; but the party convicted shall nevertheless be liable and subject to indictment, trial, judgment, and punishment, according to law.

SECTION IV.

The times, places, and manner of holding elec- *Elections, when and how held.* tions for Senators and Representatives shall be prescribed in each State by the legislature thereof ; but the Congress may at any time by law make or alter such regulations, except as to the places of choosing Senators.

The Congress shall assemble at least once in every *Congress assemble annually.* year, and such meeting shall be on the first Monday in December, unless they shall by law appoint a different day.

SECTION V.

Each house shall be the judge of the elections, *Elections, how judged.* returns, and qualifications of its own members, and a majority of each shall constitute a quorum to do *Quorum.* business ; but a smaller number may adjourn from *Absent members.* day to day, and may be authorized to compel the attendance of absent members, in such manner, and under such penalties as each house may provide.

Each house may determine the rules of its pro- *Rules.* ceedings, punish its members for disorderly behavior, *Expulsion.* and with the concurrence of two-thirds, expel a member

Each house shall keep a journal of its proceed- *Journals to be kept and publish ed.* ings, and from time to time publish the same, except such parts as may in their judgment require secrecy, *Yeas and nays.* and the yeas and nays of the members of either house on any question shall, at the desire of one-fifth of those present, be entered on the journal.

Neither house, during the session of Congress, shall without the
consent of the other, adjourn for more than three
days. nor to any other place than that in which the
two houses shall be sitting.

Adjournment.

SECTION VI.

The Senators and Representatives shall receive a compensation
for their services. to be ascertained by law, and paid
out of the Treasury of the United States. They
shall in all cases except treason, felony and breach of the peace, be
privileged from arrest during their attendance at the
session of their respective houses, and in going to
and returning from the same ; and for any speech or debate in either
house, they shall not be questioned in any other place.

Compensation.

Privileges.

No Senator or Representative shall, during the time for which he
was elected, be appointed to any civil office under
the authority of the United States, which shall have
been created, or the emoluments whereof shall have
been increased during such time ; and no person
holding any office under the United States shall be a
member of either house during his continuance in office.

*Members not ap-
pointed to office.*

*Officers of gov-
ernment can not
be members.*

SECTION VII.

All bills for raising revenue shall originate in the
House of Representatives ; but the Senate may propose or concur with amendments as on other bills.

Revenue bills.

Every bill which shall have passed the House of Representatives
and the Senate, shall, before it become a law, be
presented to the President of the United States ; if
he approve he shall sign it, but if not he shall return
it, with his objections to that house in which it shall
have originated, who shall enter the objections at
large on their journal, and proceed to reconsider it.

*Bills to be pre-
sented to the
president.*

*His powers over
them.*

*Proceedings on
his veto.*

If after such reconsideration two-thirds of that house
shall agree to pass the bill, it shall be sent, together with the objections, to the other house, by which it shall likewise be reconsidered,
and if approved by two-thirds of that house, it shall become a law.
But in all cases the votes of both houses shall be determined by yeas
and nays. and the names of the persons voting for and against the
bill shall be entered on the journal of each house respectively. If

any bill shall not be returned by the President within ten days (Sundays excepted) after it shall have been presented to him. the same shall be a law, in like manner as if he had signed it, unless the Congress by their adjournment prevent its return, in which case it shall not be a law.

Bills to be laws if not returned in ten days.

Every order, resolution, or vote to which the concurrence of the Senate and House of Representatives may be necessary (except on a question of adjournment) shall be presented to the President of the United States; and before the same shall take effect, shall be approved by him, or being disapproved by him, shall be repassed by two-thirds of the Senate and House of Representatives, according to the rules and limitations prescribed in the case of a bill.

Joint orders or resolutions to be approved by the President.

SECTION VIII.

The Congress shall have power to lay and collect taxes, duties, imposts and excises, to pay the debts and provide for the common defence and general welfare of the United States ; but all duties, imposts and excises shall be uniform throughout the United . States ;

Power of Congress to lay taxes —pay debts.

General welfare.

Duties uniform.

To borrow money on the credit of the United States ;

Borrow money.

To regulate commerce with foreign nation, and among the several States, and with the Indian tribes.

Commerce.

To establish a uniform rule of naturalization, and uniform laws on the subject of bankruptcies throughout the United States ;

Naturalization.

Bankruptcy.

To coin money, regulate the value thereof, and of foreign coin, and fix the standard of weights and measures ;

Coin money,

Weights and measures.

To provide for the punishment of counterfeiting the securities and current coin of the United States ;

Counterfeiting.

To establish post offices and post roads ;

Post roads.

To promote the progress of science and useful arts, by securing for limited times to authors and inventors the exclusive right to their respective writings and discoveries ;

Promote arts and science.

To constitute tribunals inferior to the Supreme Court ;

Inferior courts.

Piracies, &c.

To defioe and punish piracies and felonies committed on the high seas, and offences against the law of nations ;

Declare war and make captures.

To declare war, grant letters of marque and reprisal, and make rules concerning captures on land and water ;

Raise Armies.

To raise and support armies, but no approp iation of money to that use shall be for a longer term than two years ;

Navy.

To provide and maintain a navy ;

Rules and articles of war.

To make rules for the government and regulation of the land and naval forces ;

Call out militia.

To provide for calling forth the militia to execute the laws of the Union, suppress insurrections and repel invasions ;

Organize and govern militia.

Officers of militia.

To provide for organizing, arming, and disciplining the militia, and for governing such part of them as may be employed in the service of the United States, reserving to the States respectively, the appointment of the officers, and the authority of training the militia according to the discipline prescribed by Congress ;

Exclusive legislation over seat of government.

To exercise exclusive legislation in all cases whatsoever, over such district (not exceeding ten miles square) as may, by cession of particular States, and the acceptance of Congress, become the seat of the government of the United States, and to exercise like authority over all places purchased by the consent of the legislature of the State in which the same shall be, for the erection of forts, magazines, arsenals, dock-yards, and other needful buildings ; — and

And over forts, arsenals, docks, &c.

To make general laws to carry powers into effect.

To make all laws which shall be necessary and proper for carrying into execution the foregoing powers, and all other powers vested by this Constitution in the Government of the United States, or in any department or officer thereof.

SECTION IX.

Importation of slaves allowed till 1808.

The migration or importation of such persons as any of the States now existing shall think proper to admit, shall not be prohibited by the Congress prior to the year one thousand eight hundred and eight. but a tax or duty may be imposed on such importation, not exceeding ten dollars for each person.

The privilege of the writ of habeas corpus shall not be suspended, unless when in cases of rebellion or invasion the public safety may re uire it.

Habeas corpus.

No bill of attainder or ex post facto law shall be passed.

Attainder and ex post facto laws.

No capitation, or other direct tax shall be laid. unless in proportion to the census or enumeration hereinb fore directed to be taken.

Direct taxes.

No tax or duty shall be laid on articl s exported from any State

No exportation duty.

No preference shall be given by any regulation of commerce or revenue to the ports of one State over those of another: nor shall vessels bound to, or from, one State, be obliged to enter, clear, or pay duties in another.

Commerce between the States.

No money shall be drawn from the treasury, but in consequence of appropriations made by law ; and a regular statement and account of the receipts and expenditures of all public money shall be published from time to time.

Money, how drawn from the treasury.

To be published.

No title of nobility shall be granted by the United States ; and no person holding any office of profit or trust under them, shall, without the consent of the Congress, accept of any present, emolument, office, or title, of any kind whatever, from any king, prince, or foreign State.

No nobility.

Foreign presents and titles.

SECTION X.

No State shall enter into any treaty, alliance, or confederation ; grant letters of marque and reprisal ; coin money ; emit bills of credit ; make anything but gold and silver coin a tender in payment of debts ; pass any bill of attainder, ex post facto law, or law impairing the obligation of contracts, or grant any title of nobility.

Powers denied to the States.

No state shall, without the consent of the Congress lay any imposts or duties on imports or exports, ex· cept what may be absolutely necessary for executing its inspection laws ; and the net produce of all duties and imposts, laid by any State on imports or exports, shall be for the use of the Treasury of the United States ; and all such laws shall be subject to the revision and control of the Congress.

Other powers denied to States.

No State shall, without the consent of Congress. lay any duty of tonnage, keep troops, or ships of war in time of peace, enter into any agreement or compact with an-

Further denial of powers to States.

other State, or with a foreign power, or engage in war, unless actually invaded, or in such imminent danger as will not admit of delay.

ARTICLE II.

SECTION I.

President of the United States. The executive power shall be vested in a President of the United States of America. He shall hold his office during the term of four years, and together with the Vice President, chosen for the same term, be elected as follows:

Electors, how appointed. Each State shall appoint, in such manner as the legislature thereof may direct, a number of electors, equal to the whole number of Senators and Representatives to which the State may be entitled in Congress; but no Senator or Representative, or person holding an office of trust or profit under the United States, shall be appointed an elector.

Electors to meet and to elect a President and Vice President. The electors shall meet in their respective States, and vote by ballot for two persons, of whom one at least shall not be an inhabitant of the same State with themselves. And they shall make a list of all the persons voted for, and of the number of votes for each; which list they shall sign and certify, and transmit sealed to the seat of the government of the United States, directed to the President of the Senate. The President of the Senate shall, in the

Their votes counted in Congress. presence of the Senate and House of Representatives, open all the certificates, and the votes shall then be counted. The person having the greatest number of votes shall be the President, if such number be a majority of the whole number of electors appointed; and if there be more than one who have such a

Representatives to choose if electors fail. majority, and have an equal number of votes, then the House of Representatives shall immediately choose by ballot one of them for President; and if no person have a majority, then from the five highest on the list the said House shall in like manner choose the President. But in choos-

Votes by States. ing the President, the votes shall be taken by States, the representatives from each State having one vote; a quorum for this purpose shall consist of a member or members from two-thirds of the States, and a majority of all the States shall be necessary for a choice. In every case, after the choice of the

Vice President. President, the person having the greatest number of votes of the electors, shall be the Vice President.

But if there should remain two or more who have equal votes, the Senate shall choose from them by ballot the Vice President.*

The Congress may determine the time of choosing the electors, and the day on which they shall give their votes; which day shall be the same throughout the United States. Election and meeting of electors.

No person except a natural born citizen, or a citizen of the United States, at the time of the adoption Qualifications of President. of this Constitution shall be eligible to the office of President; neither shall any person be eligible to that office who shall not have attained to the age of thirty-five years, and been fourteen years a resident within the United States.

In case of the removal of the President from office, or of his death, resignation, or inability, to Removal, dea'h. &c., of President. discharge the powers and duties of the said office, the same shall devolve on the Vice President, and the Congress may by law provide for the case of removal, death, resignation, or inability, both of the President and Vice President, declaring what officer shall then act as President, and such officer shall then act accordingly, until the disability be removed, or a President shall be elected.

The President shall, at stated times, receive for his services a compensation, which shall neither be Compensation of President. increased nor diminished during the period for which he shall have been elected, and he shall not receive within that period any other emolument from the United States, or any of them.

Before he enter on the execution of his office, he shall take the following oath or affirmation:—

"I do solemnly swear (or affirm) that I will faith- Oath. fully execute the office of President of the United States. and will to the best of my ability preserve, protect, and defend the Constitution of the United States "

SECTION II.

The President shall be Commander-in-chief of the army and navy of the United States, and of the Powers and duties of the President. militia of the several States, when called into the actual service of the United States ; he may require the opinion, in writing, of the principal officer in each of the executive departments, upon any subject relating to the duties of their respective offices, and he shall have

* This clause of the Constitution has been amended. See twelfth article of the amendments, page 195.

power to grant reprieves and pardons for offences against the United States, except in cases of impeachment.

He shall have power, by and with the advice and consent of the Senate, to make treaties, provided two thirds of the senators present concur; and he shall nominate, and, by and with the advice and consent of the Senate, shall appoint, ambassadors, other public ministers and consuls, judges of the Supreme Court, and all other officers of the United States, whose appointments are not herein otherwise provided for, and which shall be established by law ; but the Congress may by law vest the appointment of such inferior officers, as they think proper, in the President alone, in the courts of law, or in the heads of departments.

Appointment of public officers.

The President shall have power to fill up all vacancies that may happen during the recess of the Senate, by granting commissions which shall expire at the end of their next session.

Vacancies in office.

SECTION III.

He shall from time to time give to the Congress information of the state of the Union, and recommend to their consideration such measures as he shall judge necessary and expedient ; he may, on extraordinary occasions, convene both houses, or either of them, and in case of disagreement between them, with respect to the time of adjournment, he may adjourn them to such time as he shall think proper ; he shall receive ambassadors and other public ministers ; he shall take care that the laws be faithfully executed, and shall commission all the officers of the United States.

Further powers and duties of the President.

SECTION IV.

The President, Vice President, and all civil officers of the United States, shall be removed from office on impeachment for, and conviction of treason, bribery, or other high crimes and misdemeanors.

Impeachment.

ARTICLE III.

SECTION I.

The judicial power of the United States shall be vested in one Supreme Court, and in such inferior courts as the Congress may from time to time ordain and establish.

Judiciary and tenure of judges.

The judges, both of the Supreme and inferior courts, shall hold their offices during good behavior, and shall, at stated times, receive for their services a compensation which shall not be diminished during their continuance in office.

SECTION II.

The judicial power shall extend to all cases, in law and equity, arising under this Constitution, the *Power of the judiciary.* laws of the United States, and treaties made, or which shall be made, under their authority ;—to all cases affecting ambassadors, other public ministers, and consuls ; to all cases of admiralty and maritime jurisdiction ; to controversies to which the United States shall be a party ; to controversies between two or more States ; between a State and citizens of another State ; between citizens of different States ; between citizens of the same State claiming lands under grants of different States, and between a State, or the citizens thereof, and foreign States, citizens or subjects.

In all cases affecting ambassadors, or other public ministers and consuls, and those in which a State shall be a party, the Supreme Court shall have *Jurisdiction of the Supreme Court.* original jurisdiction. In all the other cases before mentioned, the Supreme Court shall have appellate jurisdiction, both as to law and fact, with such exceptions, and under such regulations as the Congress shall make.

The trial of all crimes, except in cases of im- *Trials by jury.* peachment, shall be by jury ; and such trial shall be *And where held.* held in the State where the said crimes shall have been committed ; but when not committed within any State, the trial shall be at such place or places as the Congress may by law have directed.

SECTION III.

Treason against the United States shall consist *Treason.* only in levying war against them, or in adhering to their enemies, giving them aid and comfort. No person shall be convicted of treason unless on the testimony of two witnesses to the same overt act, or on confession in open court.

The Congress shall have power to declare the punishment of treason, but no attainder of treason *No corruption of blood.* shall work corruption of blood or forfeiture except during the life of the person attainted.

ARTICLE IV.

SECTION I.

Acts of States accredited.

Full faith and credit shall be given in each State to the public acts, records, and judicial proceedings of every other State. And the Congress may by general laws prescribe the manner in which such acts, records and proceedings shall be proved, and the effect thereof.

SECTION II.

Privileges of citizenship.

The citizens of each State shall be entitled to all privileges and immunities of citizens in the several States.

Fugitives from justice to be delivered up.

A person charged in any State with treason, felony, or other crime, who shall flee from justice, and be found in another State, shall, on demand of the executive authority of the State from which he fled, be delivered up, to be removed to the State having jurisdiction of the crime.

Fugitive slaves to be delivered up.

No person held to service or labor in one State, under the laws thereof, escaping into another, shall, in consequence of any law or regulation therein, be discharged from such service or labor, but shall be delivered up on claim of the party to whom such service or labor may be due.

SECTION III.

New States

New States may be admitted by the Congress into this Union ; but no new State shall be formed or erected within the jurisdiction of any other State ; nor any State be formed by the junction of two or more States, or part of States, without the consent of the legislatures of the States concerned as well as of the Congress.

Territory and other property of United States.

The Congress shall have power to dispose of and make all needful rules and regulations respecting the territory or other property belonging to the United States ; and nothing in this Constitution shall be so construed as to prejudice any claims of the United States, or of any particular State.

SECTION IV.

Republican form of government.

The United States shall guaranty to every State in this Union a republican form of government, and shall protect each of them against invasion, and on Protection of States. application of the legislature, or of the executive, (when the legislature cannot be convened,) against domestic violence.

ARTICLE V.

The Congress, whenever two-thirds of both houses Amendments of the Constitution. shall deem it necessary, shall propose amendments to this Constitution, or, on the application of the legislatures of two-thirds of the several States, shall call a convention for proposing amendments, which in either case, shall be valid to all intents and purposes, as part of this Constitution, when ratified by the legislatures of three-fourths of the several States, or by conventions in three-fourths thereof, as the one or the other mode of ratification may be proposed by the Congress; provided that no amendment which may be made prior to the year one thousand eight hundred and eight, shall in any manner affect the first and fourth clauses in the ninth section of the first article; and that no State, without its consent, shall be deprived of its equal suffrage in the Senate.

ARTICLE VI.

All debts contracted and engagements entered Debts of former government recognized. into, before the adoption of this Constitution, shall be as valid against the United States under this Constitution as under the confederation.

This Constitution, and the laws of the United What constitutes the supreme law. States which shall be made in pursuance thereof, and all treaties made, or which shall be made, under the authority of the United States, shall be the supreme law of the land; and the judges in every State shall be bound thereby, anything in the Constitution or laws of any State to the contrary notwithstanding.

The Senators and Representatives before men- Oath of public officers. tioned, and the members of the several State legislatures, and all executive and judicial officers, both of the United States and of the several States, shall be bound by oath or affirmation, to support this Constitution; but no religious test shall ever be required as a qualification to any No religious test. office or public trust under the United States.

ARTICLE VII.

Ratification.   The ratification of the conventions of nine States shall be sufficient for the establishment of this Constitution between the States so ratifying the same.

Done in convention by the unanimous consent of the States present the seventeenth day of September in the year of our Lord one thousand seven hundred and eighty seven and of the Independence of the United States of America the twelfth. In witness whereof we have hereunto subscribed our names.

GEO. WASHINGTON—
Presid't and deputy from Virginia.

NEW HAMPSHIRE.
John Langdon,
Nicholas Gilman.

MASSACHUSETTS.
Nathaniel Gorham,
Rufus King.

CONNECTICUT.
Wm. Saml. Johnson,
Roger Sherman.

NEW YORK.
Alexander Hamilton.

NEW JERSEY.
Wil. Livingston,
David Brearley,
Wm. Paterson,
Jona. Dayton.

PENNSYLVANIA.
B. Franklin,
Thomas Mifflin,
Robt. Morris,
Geo. Clymer,
Tho. Fitzsimons,
Jared Ingersoll,
James Wilson,
Gouv. Morris.

DELAWARE.
Geo. Read,
Gunning Bedford, jun'r,
John Dickinson.
Richard Bassett,
Jaco. Broom.

MARYLAND.
James McHenry,
Dan. of St. Thos. Jenifer,
Danl. Carroll.

VIRGINIA.
John Blair,
James Madison, jr.

NORTH CAROLINA.
Wm. Blount,
Rich'd Dobbs Spaight.
Hu. Williamson.

SOUTH CAROLINA.
J. Rutledge,
Charles Coatesworth Pinckney,
Charles Pinckney,
Pierce Butler.

GEORGIA.
William Few,
Abr. Baldwin.

Attest :   WILLIAM JACKSON, *Secretary.*

AMENDMENTS TO THE CONSTITUTION.

ARTICLE I.

Congress shall make no law respecting an establishment of religion, or prohibiting the free exercise thereof ; or abridging the freedom of speech, or of the press ; or the right of the people peaceably to assemble, and to petition the government for a redress of grievances.

No State religion.

Freedom of speech and the press.

Right of petition.

ARTICLE II.

A well regulated militia, being necessary to the security of a free State, the right of the people to keep and bear arms shall not be infringed.

State militia.

ARTICLE III.

No soldier shall, in time of peace, be quartered in any house, without the consent of the owner, nor in time of war, but in a manner to be prescribed by law.

Billeting soldiers on citizens.

ARTICLE IV.

The right of the people to be secure in their persons, houses, papers, and effects, against unreasonable searches and seizures, shall not be violated, and no warrants shall issue, but upon probable cause, supported by oath or affirmation, and particularly describing the place to be searched, and the persons or things to be seized.

Rights of domicile and person.

ARTICLE V.

No person shall be held to answer for a capital or otherwise infamous crime, unless on a presentment or indictment of a grand jury, except in cases arising in the land or naval forces, or in the militia, when in actual service in time of war or public danger ; nor shall any person be subject for the same offense to be twice put in jeopardy of life or limb ; nor shall be compelled in any criminal case to be a witness against himself, nor be deprived of

Holding for crime limited.

Testifying against self not to be compelled.

Right of private property inviolable.

life, liberty, or property. without due process of law; nor shall private property be taken for public use, without just compensation.

ARTICLE VI.

Right of jury trial, etc , in criminal cases.

In all criminal prosecutions, the accused shall enjoy the right to a speedy and public trial, by an impartial jury of the State and district wherein the crime shall have been committed, which district shall have been previously ascertained by law, and to be informed of the nature and cause of the accusation ; to be confronted with the witnesses against him ; to have compulsory process for obtaining witnesses in his favor, and to have the assistance of counsel for his defence.

ARTICLE VII.

Jury trial in civil cases.

In suits at common law, where the value in controversy shall exceed twenty dollars, the right of trial by jury shall be preserved, and no fact tried by a jury shall be otherwise re-examined in any court of the United States, than according to the rules of the common law.

ARTICLE VIII.

Bail, fines and punishments not excessive.

Excessive bail shall not be required, nor excessive fines imposed, nor cruel and unusual punishments inflicted.

ARTICLE IX.

Rights reserved by people.

The enumeration in the Constitution, of certain rights, shall not be construed to deny or disparage others retained by the people.

ARTICLE X.

Rights reserved by States and people.

The powers not delegated to the United States by the Constitution, nor prohibited by it to the States, are reserved to the States respectively, or to the people.

ARTICLE XI.

Suits against States.

The judicial power of the United States shall not be construed to extend to any suit in law or equity, commenced or prosecuted against one of the United States by citizens of another State. or by citizens or subjects of any foreign State.

ARTICLE XII.

The electors shall meet in their respective States and vote by ballot for President and Vice President, one of whom, at least, shall not be an inhabitant of the same State with themselves ; they shall name in their ballots the person voted for as President, and in distinct ballots the person voted for as Vice President, and they shall make distinct lists of all persons voted for as President, and of all persons voted for as Vice President, and of the number of votes for each ; which lists they shall sign and certify, and transmit sealed to the seat of government of the United States, directed to the President of the Senate. The President of the Senate shall, in the presence of the Senate and House of Representatives, open all the certificates and the votes shall then be counted ;— the person having the greatest number of votes for President, shall be the President, if such number be a majority of the whole number of electors appointed ; and if no person have such a majority, then from the persons having the highest numbers not exceeding three on the list of those voted for as President, the House of Representatives shall choose immediately, by ballot, the President. But in choosing the President, the votes shall be taken by States, the representation from each State having one vote ; a quorum for this purpose shall consist of a member or members from two thirds of the States, and a majority of all the States shall be necessary to a choice. And if the House of Representatives shall not choose a President whenever the right of choice shall devolve upon them, before the fourth day of March, next following, then the Vice President shall act as President, as in the case of the death or other constitutional disability of the President.

Electing President and Vice President.

The person having the greatest number of votes as Vice President, shall be the Vice President, if such number be a majority of the whole number of electors appointed, and if no person have a majority, then from the two highest numbers on the list, the Senate shall choose the Vice President ; a quorum for the purpose shall consist of two thirds of the whole number of Senators, and a majority of the whole number shall be necessary to a choice. But no person constitutionally ineligible to the office of President shall be eligible to that of Vice President of the United States.

ARTICLE XIII.

SECTION 1. Neither slavery nor involuntary servitude, except as a punishment for crime, whereof

Slavery prohibited.

the party shall have been duly convicted, shall exist within the United States, or any place subject to their jurisdiction.

SECTION 2. Congress shall have power to enforce this article by appropriate legislation.

ARTICLE XIV.

Civil rights.

SECTION 1. All persons born or naturalized in the United States, and subject to the jurisdiction thereof, are citizens of the United States, and of the State wherein they reside. No State shall make or enforce any law which shall abridge the privileges and immunities of citizens of the United States. Nor shall any State deprive any person of life, liberty or property without due process of law, nor to deny to any person within its jurisdiction the equal protection of the laws.

Basis of Congressional representation.

SEC. 2. Representatives shall be apportioned among the several States according to their respective numbers, counting the whole number of persons in each State, excluding Indians not taxed ; but whenever the right to vote at any election for electors of President and Vice President, or United States Representatives in Congress, executive and judicial officers, or the members of the Legislature thereof, is denied to any of the male inhabitants of such State, being twenty-one years of age, and citizens of the United States, or in any way abridged, except for participation in rebellion or other crimes, the basis of representation therein shall be reduced in the proportion which the number of such male citizens shall bear to the whole number of male citizens twenty-one years of age in that State.

Disqualification for office.

SEC. 3 No person shall be a Senator or Representative in Congress, elector of President and Vice President, or hold any office, civil or military, under the United States, or under any State, who, having previously taken an oath as a member of Congress, or as an officer of the United States, or as a member of any State Legislature, or as an executive or judicial officer of any State, to support the Constitution of the United States, shall have engaged in insurrection or rebellion against the same, or given aid or comfort to the enemies thereof ; but Congress may, by a vote of two thirds of each House, remove such disability.

National debt — debts in aid of rebellion.

SEC. 4. The validity of the public debt of the United States authorized by law, including debts incurred for the payment of pensions and bounties for service in suppressing insurrection or rebellion, shall not be questioned ; but neither the United States nor any State shall assume to pay any debt or obligation incurred in aid of insurrection or rebellion against the United States, or any claim for the loss or emancipation of any slave, but all such debts, obligations, and claims shall be illegal and void.

SEC. 5. The Congress shall have power to enforce, by appropriate legislation, the provisions of this article.

ARTICLE XV.

SECTION 1. The right of citizens of the United States to vote shall not be denied or abridged by the United States, or by any State, on account of race, color or previous condition of servitude.

SEC. 2. The Congress shall have power to enforce this article by appropriate legislation.

DECLARATION OF INDEPENDENCE.

A DECLARATION BY THE REPRESENTATIVES OF THE UNITED
STATES OF AMERICA, IN CONGRESS ASSEMBLED,
JULY 4, 1776.

WHEN, in the course of human events, it becomes necessary for
one people to dissolve the political bands which have connected them
with another, and to assume, among the powers of the earth, the
separate and equal station to which the laws of nature and of nature's
God entitle them, a decent respect to the opinions of mankind requires
that they should declare the causes which impel them to the separation.

We hold these truths to be self-evident—that all men are created
equal ; that they are endowed by their Creator with certain unalien-
able rights; that among these are life, liberty, and the pursuit of
happiness ; that, to secure these rights, governments are instituted
among men, deriving their just powers from the consent of the
governed ; that, whenever any form of government becomes destruc-
tive of these ends, it is the right of the people to alter or abolish it,
and to institute a new government, laying its foundation on such
principles, and organizing its powers in such form, as to them shall
seem most likely to effect their safety and happiness. Prudence,
indeed, will dictate that governments long established should not be
changed for light and transient causes ; and, accordingly, all experience has shown that mankind are more disposed to suffer, while
evils are sufferable, than to right themselves by abolishing the forms
to which they are accustomed. But when a long train of abuses and
usurpations, pursuing invariably the same object, evinces a design to
reduce them under absolute despotism, it is their right, it is their
duty to throw off such government, and to provide new guards for
their future security.

Such has been the patient sufferance of these colonies, and such
is now the necessity which constrains them to alter their former system of government. The history of the present king of Great
Britain is a history of repeated injuries and usurpations, all having,

in direct object, the establishment of an absolute tyranny over these states. To prove this let facts be submitted to a candid world :

He has refused his assent to laws the most wholesome and necessary for the public good.

He has forbidden his governors to pass laws of immediate and pressing importance, unless suspended in their operation until his assent should be obtained ; and, when so suspended, he has utterly neglected to attend to them.

He has refused to pass other laws for the accommodation of large districts of people, unless those people would relinquish the right of representation in the Legislature — a right inestimable to them, and formidable to tyrants only.

He has called together legislative bodies at places unusual, uncomfortable, and distant from the depository of their public records, for the sole purpose of fatiguing them into compliance with his measures.

He has dissolved representative houses repeatedly for opposing with manly firmness his invasions on the rights of the people.

He has refused, for a long time after such dissolution, to cause others to be elected whereby the legislative powers, incapable of annihilation, have returned to the people at large for their exercise ; the state remaining. in the mean time, exposed to all the dangers of invasion from without and convulsions within.

He has endeavored to prevent the population of these states ; for that purpose obstructing the laws for naturalization of foreigners, refusing to pass others to encourage their migration hither and raising the conditions of new appropriations of lands

He has obstructed the administration of justice by refusing his assent to laws for establishing judiciary powers.

He has made judges dependent on his will alone for the tenure of their offices, and the amount and payment of their salaries.

He has erected a multitude of new offices, and sent hither swarms of officers to harass our people and eat out their substance.

He has kept among us, in times of peace, standing armies without the consent of our Legislature.

He has affected to render the military independent of and superior to the civil power.

He has combined with others to subject us to a jurisdiction foreign to our Constitution, and unacknowledged by our laws, giving his assent to their acts of pretended legislation ;

For quartering large bodies of armed troops among us:

For protecting them, by a mock trial, from punishment for any murders which they should commit on the inhabitants of these states :

For cutting off our trade with all parts of the world :

For imposing taxes on us without our consent :

For depriving us, in many cases, of the benefits of trial by jury :

For transporting us beyond seas to be tried for pretended offences :

For abolishing the free system of English laws in a neighboring province, establishing therein an arbitrary government, and enlarging its boundaries, so as to render it at once an example and fit instrument for introducing the same absolute rule into these colonies :

For taking away our charters, abolishing our most valuable laws, and altering fundamentally the powers of our governments :

For suspending our own Legislatures, and declaring themselves invested with power to legislate for us in all cases whatsoever.

He has abdicated government here by declaring us out of his protection, and waging war against us.

He has plundered our seas, ravaged our coasts, burnt our towns, and destroyed the lives of our people.

He is, at this time, transporting large armies of foreign mercenaries to complete the works of death, desolation, and tyranny, already begun, with circumstances of cruelty and perfidy scarcely paralleled in the most barbarous ages, and totally unworthy the head of a civilized nation.

He has constrained our fellow-citizens, taken captive on the high seas, to bear arms against their country, to become the executioners of their friends and brethren, or to fall themselves by their hands.

He has excited domestic insurrections amongst us, and has endeavored to bring on the inhabitants of our frontiers the merciless Indian savages, whose known rule of warfare is an undistinguished destruction of all ages, sexes, and conditions.

In every stage of these oppressions, we have petitioned for redress in the most humble terms ; our repeated petitions have been answered only by repeated injury. A prince whose character is thus marked by every act which may define a tyrant is unfit to be the ruler of a free people.

Nor have we been wanting in attention to our British brethren. We have warned them, from time to time, of attempts made by their Legislature to extend an unwarrantable jurisdiction over us. We have reminded them of the circumstances of our emigration and settlement here. We have appealed to their native justice and magnanimity, and we have conjured them, by the ties of our common kindred, to disavow these usurpations, which would inevitably interrupt our connections and correspondence. They, too, have been deaf to the voice of justice and consanguinity. We must, therefore, acquiesce in the necessity which denounces our separation, and hold them, as we hold the rest of mankind — enemies in war, in peace friends.

We, therefore, the representatives of the United States of America, in General Congress assembled, appealing to the Supreme Judge of the world for the rectitude of our intentions, do, in the name and by the authority of the good people of these colonies, solemnly publish and declare that these United States are, and of right ought to be, free and independent states ; that they are absolved from all allegiance to the British crown, and that all political connection between them and the state of Great Britain is, and ought to be, totally dissolved ; and that, as free and independent states, they have full power to levy war, conclude peace, contract alliances, establish commerce, and to do all other acts and things which independent states may of right do. And for the support of this declaration, with a firm reliance on the protection of Divine Providence, we mutually pledge to each other our lives, our fortunes, and our sacred honor.

The foregoing declaration was, by order of Congress, engrossed, and signed by the following members :   JOHN HANCOCK.

> *New Hampshire.*—Josiah Bartlett, William Whipple, Matthew Thornton.
> *Massachusetts Bay*—Samuel Adams, John Adams, Robert Treat Paine, Elbridge Gerry.
> *Rhode Island.*—Stephen Hopkins, William Ellery.
> *Connecticut.*—Roger Sherman, Samuel Huntington, William Williams, Oliver Wolcott.
> *New York.*—William Floyd, Philip Livingston, Francis Lewis, Lewis Morris.
> *New Jersey.*—Richard Stockton, John Witherspoon, Francis Hopkinson, John Hart, Abraham Clark.
> *Pennsylvania*—Robert Morris, Benjamin Rush, Benjamin Franklin, John Morton, George Clymer, James Smith, George Taylor, James Wilson, George Ross.
> *Delaware.*—Cæsar Rodney, George Read, Thomas M'Kean.
> *Maryland.*—Samuel Chase, William Paca, Thomas Stone, Charles Carroll, of Carrollton.
> *Virginia*—George Wythe, Richard Henry Lee, Thomas Jefferson, Benjamin Harrison, Thomas Nelson, Jr., Francis Lightfoot Lee, Carter Braxton.
> *North Carolina*—William Hooper, Joseph Hewes, John Penn.
> *South Carolina*—Edward Rutledge, Thomas Heyward, Jr., Thomas Lynch, Jr., Arthur Middleton.
> *Georgia.*—Button Gwinnett, Lyman Hall, George Walton.